W0469570

Mini Pies

Mini Pies

LOVE FOOD™

This edition published in 2012

LOVE FOOD is an imprint of Parragon Books Ltd

Parragon
Chartist House
15-17 Trim Street
Bath BA1 1HA, UK

Copyright © Parragon Books Ltd 2011

LOVE FOOD and the accompanying heart device is a registered trade mark of Parragon Books Ltd in Australia, the UK, USA, India and the EU.

www.parragon.com/lovefood

All rights reserved.. No part of this publication may be reproduced, stored in a retrieval system or transmitted, in any form or by any means, electronic, mechanical, photocopying, recording or otherwise, without the prior permission of the copyright holder.

ISBN 978-1-4454-8747-2

Printed in China

Created and produced by Pene Parker and Becca Spry
Author and home economist: Sara Lewis
Photographer: Noel Murphy

Notes for the Reader
This book uses both metric and imperial measurements. Follow the same units of measurement throughout; do not mix metric and imperial. All spoon measurements are level: teaspoons are assumed to be 5 ml, and tablespoons are assumed to be 15 ml. Unless otherwise stated, milk is assumed to be full fat, eggs and individual vegetables are medium, and pepper is freshly ground black pepper. Unless otherwise stated, all root vegetables should be washed and peeled prior to using.

Garnishes, decorations and serving suggestions are all optional and not necessarily included in the recipe ingredients or method.

The times given are an approximate guide only. Preparation times differ according to the techniques used by different people and the cooking times may also vary from those given. Optional ingredients, variations or serving suggestions have not been included in the time calculations.

Recipes using raw or very lightly cooked eggs should be avoided by infants, the elderly, pregnant women, convalescents and anyone suffering from an illness. Pregnant and breastfeeding women are advised to avoid eating peanuts and peanut products. Sufferers from nut allergies should be aware that some of the ready-made ingredients used in the recipes in this book may contain nuts. Always check the packaging before use.

Contents

Introduction

These bite-sized pies, made with buttery crumbly pastry, will melt in your mouth. There are tiny pies that are ideal for parties and slightly larger pies that are delicious for a light lunch or dessert. There's something for everyone, from pies made with shortcrust to crunchy biscuit crumb cases and wafer-thin filo delights.

Muffin tins
Tins come with 6, 12 and 24 sections. If using a 6- or 12-section tin you will need to bake 2 or more batches of pies for some of the recipes in this book. Metal tins with a non-stick finish are best, as the metal conducts heat efficiently, producing a crisp crust. Different grades and prices are available. Silicone muffin tins are best kept for muffins and cakes rather than for more fragile pie crusts.

Cookie cutters
You will need a 10-cm/4-inch plain or fluted cookie cutter for the muffin-sized pies and a 6-cm/2½-inch cutter for the mini muffin sized pies, plus slightly smaller cutters for the pie tops. If you don't have the right size, check the tops of your glasses, cups and saucers and cut around these. It is worth buying cookie cutters with different shaped edges and finishes, including tiny novelty shaped cutters such as hearts, flowers, stars, letters and holly leaves.

Cutters for pastry decorations
Make pie lids from flower, heart or circle shapes stamped out with cookie cutters – use these instead of round lids. You can also stamp out tiny versions of these shapes using mini cookie cutters and stick them to your round pastry lid using milk. If you don't have any cutters, cut leaves freehand with a sharp knife.

Pastry wheel
This looks a bit like a scaled-down version of a pizza cutter; buy one with a fluted edge for cutting strips of pastry for lattice-topped pies.

Pastry brushes
Use a clean brush with firmly attached bristles. Ideally have two different-sized ones, one slightly smaller than the other, for glazing and brushing the top edges of the mini muffin sized pies. Wash your brushes after use in warm soapy water and dry well before storing.

Oven thermometers
Ovens vary greatly in their accuracy, with some fan ovens being very hot. Monitor your oven with a small oven thermometer; they are inexpensive and widely available from cookshops and hardware stores. Simply hang the thermometer from a shelf so it reads the temperature in the centre of your oven.

The importance of chilling pastry
Chilling the pastry after making it enables the dough to relax and so minimizes the chances of it shrinking during cooking. Shrinkage is most obvious when making a single crust pie that is baked blind. Well chilled pastry is also much easier to roll out.

Baking blind
'Baking blind' means to bake a pie or tart without a filling, and it is done to stop the filling from soaking through the pastry during cooking and producing a soggy-bottomed pie. Soggy pastry not only affects the taste of the pie, but also makes it hard to remove it from the tin. Roll out and line sections of a muffin tin with pastry, then prick the base with a fork once or twice and chill again for 15 minutes. Line the pastry with baking paper a little larger than the tin (crumple the paper up before using to make it easier to fit). Half-fill with baking beans (available from cookshops), small dried pasta

shapes or dried pulses, to keep the pastry in shape for muffin sized pie cases. Bake at 190°C/375°F/Gas Mark 5 for 10 minutes, then remove the paper and beans and cook for 2–3 minutes more, until the cases are crisp and dry. Allow the beans, pasta or pulses to cool, then store them. Add the filling to the pies and continue to cook as per the recipe. Mini muffin sized pies are so tiny that they don't need baking blind.

How to tell if a pie is cooked

Cooking times are given as a guide, but it is wise to check on the progress of your pies during baking. If your oven seems too hot and your pies are browning too quickly, protect the tops with a piece of foil or reduce the temperature slightly. Your pies may look ready on the top, but it is important that the bottom crust is also cooked through.

Ready-made shortcrust pastry

While it's great to make your own shortcrust pastry, sometimes there just isn't the time. Keep a supply of ready-made shortcrust or pie dough in the freezer, or buy it from the chiller cabinet in the supermarket.

Filo pastry

Ready-made wafer-thin filo pastry is so good that it isn't worth making your own. Packs vary in size, but if buying frozen you will need to defrost the whole pack. Separate the sheets, use as many as you need, then wrap the rest in clingfilm, put them back in the box and refreeze. (This product is the only exception to the rule about not refreezing – it is perfectly safe to do so, providing it is out of the freezer for the minimum time.) If the sheet sizes are different to those specified in the recipes, keep to the size of the trimmed squares/rectangles specified. Filo pastry is so thin that it dries out very quickly, so don't unwrap it until the very last minute and ideally unfold sheets so that they are flat, then cover them with clingfilm and just remove 1 sheet at a time as you cut and shape it.

Lattice pastry decorations

Cut ultra-thin or finger-width strips of pastry with a small knife or fluted-edged pastry wheel and either arrange over the pies in 2 layers or interweave different strips for a basketweave effect. Symmetrically arranged strips add form, while randomly arranged strips at converging angles add a more modern twist.

Crimped edges

Decorate the edges of double-crust pies by placing your finger and thumb close together, then drawing the edge of the pastry inwards with the blade of a small knife to give a scalloped edge.

Forked edges

A quick, homely finish can be made by pressing the tines of a fork against the edges of a double-crust pie.

Different toppings

Pies don't have to be topped with pastry; sprinkle with crumble, flapjack or granola or whirls of soft meringue. Add whipped cream to cooled pies and drizzle with toffee, melted chocolate, honey or maple syrup.

Egg yolk and water glaze

Beat 1 egg yolk with 1 tablespoon of cold water, then brush this over the tops of the pies using a pastry brush. This produces a burnished gold-topped glaze. Sprinkle with a little sugar before baking if you wish. Traditional cooks used to say that an egg yolk glaze should only be used for savoury pies, but you can use it for sweet if you wish.

Egg white and caster sugar glaze

This produces a more traditional, paler-coloured finish for sweet pies. Brush the tops with a little egg white, then sprinkle with caster sugar before baking.

Milk and caster sugar glaze

This produces a paler coloured finish for sweet pies, not dissimilar to the egg white and sugar glaze above. Brush the tops with a little milk, then sprinkle with caster sugar before baking. For a caramelized sugar glaze if you are making an open-topped pie, dot the fruit with a little butter and sprinkle with sugar; dust heavily with sifted icing sugar towards the end of cooking and return to the oven for the last 5 minutes, until the sugar has dissolved and caramelized to a deep golden colour.

Shortcrust pastry or pie dough

Makes: 625 g/1 lb 6 oz, or enough for 12 muffin sized pies, or 1 quantity
Prep: 25 minutes

350 g/12 oz plain flour, plus extra for dusting

55 g/2 oz caster sugar, optional

85 g/3 oz unsalted butter, chilled and diced

85 g/3 oz vegetable shortening, chilled and diced

4–4½ tbsp cold water

1

2

The most versatile, everyday pastry, this is great for sweet pies – or simply omit the sugar for savoury tarts. Mix by hand or blitz in a food processor. The key is to use just enough water to bind the pastry for a wonderful crumbly texture that melts in the mouth.

1. To make by hand: put the flour and sugar (if making sweet shortcrust) in a mixing bowl, then add the butter and shortening. Toss together, then lift the mixture and rub it through your fingers and thumbs. Continue scooping up the mixture and rubbing until it looks like breadcrumbs. Gradually mix in the water with a round-bladed knife, then squeeze the mixture together with your hands until it forms a smooth dough.

To make with an electric mixer or food processor: put the flour, sugar, butter and shortening in a bowl and mix together using the electric mixer, or add to a processor bowl fitted with a plastic or metal blade and mix briefly. It should resemble breadcrumbs. Gradually add the water with the machine running and mix briefly until it just comes together in a ball.

2. Wrap the pastry in clingfilm or put it into a small plastic bag, and chill in the fridge for 15 minutes. Knead the pastry lightly on a surface dusted with flour, then roll it out thinly. Using a plain or fluted cookie cutter, stamp out circles 10 cm/4 inches in diameter and use to line a 12-section deep muffin tin. Alternatively stamp out circles 6 cm/2½ inches in diameter and use to line 2 x 12-section mini muffin tins. When you can cut no more circles, squeeze the trimmings into a ball, then reroll this out and cut round lids, strips for lattice tops or tiny shapes.

Tips

Keep everything as cold as possible. Use butter and vegetable shortening straight from the fridge. If your hands feel hot, rinse them in cold water before you begin. Use cold water to bind. A marble pastry board is useful (but not essential) for keeping the pastry cold while rolling out.

Don't add too much liquid. Use just enough to bind the crumbs.
For shortcrust/pie dough you need 1 teaspoon of water for every 25 g/1 oz of mixture. For larger quantities change to tablespoons (1 tablespoon = 3 teaspoons). If you use too much water, the pastry will be hard.

Avoid over-flouring the work surface. Aim for the lightest of dustings and rub a little flour over the rolling pin. Before turning the pastry, loosen it with a long flexible palette knife.

All butter pastry

Makes: 650 g/1 lb 7 oz, or enough for 12 muffin sized pies, or 1 quantity
Prep: 25 minutes

350 g/12 oz plain flour, plus extra for dusting

85 g/3 oz icing sugar

175 g/6 oz unsalted butter, at room temperature, diced

4 egg yolks

1

2

Based on French 'pâte sucrée', this pastry has a higher ratio of sugar than shortcrust, is made with all butter and bound with egg yolks for richness.

1. To make by hand: spoon the flour on to the work surface, then sprinkle the sugar over the top. Mix together, then make a well in the centre and add the butter and yolks. Work the butter and yolks together with the fingers of one hand. Gradually draw in a little flour, working your fingertips in a circular motion but being careful not to let the yolk escape through the flour; use your other hand to flick a little flour around the edges so the yolks stay contained. Blend until almost of the flour has been incorporated, then knead in the last bits until you have a smooth ball.

To make with an electric mixer or food processor: put the sugar and butter in a bowl and mix together using the electric mixer, or add to a processor bowl fitted with a plastic or metal blade and mix briefly. Add the egg yolks and a little of the flour and beat until smooth, then add the remaining flour and mix to make a smooth dough.

2. Wrap in clingfilm or put into a small plastic bag, chill in the fridge for 15 minutes, then roll out and shape as in point 2 of the method on page 8.

Tips

This pastry requires careful handling. Always chill it when it is first made, and again when it is shaped. If it is too soft to roll out, roll it out thinly between 2 sheets of baking paper.

Variations for Shortcrust and All butter pastry

Cinnamon:	Add 1 teaspoon of ground cinnamon with the sugar.
Chocolate:	Make with 325 g/11½ oz plain flour and 25 g/1 oz sifted cocoa powder.
Hazelnut:	Toast 55 g/2 oz hazelnuts until golden. Chop them finely and add with the sugar.
Herb:	Omit the sugar, add 2 tablespoons of chopped fresh rosemary, parsley or chives and salt and pepper.
Lemon/Orange:	Add grated rind of 1 lemon or orange with the sugar.
Mustard:	Omit the sugar, add 2 teaspoons of dry English mustard powder and a little salt and pepper.

Party Pies

Summer fruit pies

Makes: 24 mini muffin sized pies
Prep: 30 minutes
Cook: 15 minutes

- a little butter, for greasing
- 350 g/12 oz mixed strawberries, raspberries and redcurrants
- 2 tsp cornflour
- 3 tbsp caster sugar, plus extra for sprinkling
- grated rind of ½ lemon
- 450 g/1 lb Sweet Shortcrust Pastry (see page 8) or ready-made sweet shortcrust pastry, chilled
- a little plain flour, for dusting
- 1 egg yolk mixed with 1 tbsp water, to glaze
- whipped cream, to serve

Celebrate the summer with these gorgeous red fruit pies. The soft fruit contrasts deliciously with the crisp pastry.

1. Preheat the oven to 180°C/350°F/Gas Mark 4. Lightly grease 2 x 12-section mini muffin tins.

2. Roughly chop the strawberries and break up large raspberries. Put all the fruit in a mixing bowl and stir in the cornflour, sugar and lemon rind.

3. Roll the pastry out thinly on a lightly floured surface. Using a fluted cookie cutter, stamp out 24 circles, each 6 cm/2½ inches in diameter. Press these gently into the prepared tins, rerolling the trimmings as needed. Reserve some of the trimmings for decoration.

4. Brush the top edges of the pie cases with a little of the egg glaze, then spoon in the filling.

5. Roll the reserved pastry out thinly on a lightly floured surface. Cut strips 1 cm/½ inch wide. Arrange 2 strips over each pie, pressing the edges together well to seal, then use a cookie cutter to cut small stars and arrange these over the strips. Brush egg glaze over the pastry and sprinkle with a little sugar.

6. Bake in the preheated oven for 15 minutes, or until golden. Leave to cool in the tins for 10 minutes, then loosen with a round-bladed knife and transfer to a wire rack to cool. Serve warm or cold with whipped cream.

2

5

Valentine berry love pies

Makes: 24 mini muffin sized pies
Prep: 30 minutes
Cook: 15 minutes

- a little butter, for greasing
- 350 g/12 oz strawberries
- 2 tsp cornflour
- 2 tbsp strawberry jam
- grated rind of 2 limes
- 450 g/1 lb All Butter Pastry (see page 9) or ready-made sweet shortcrust pastry, chilled
- a little plain flour, for dusting
- 1 egg yolk mixed with 1 tbsp water, to glaze
- a little caster sugar, for sprinkling

TO SERVE

- 225 ml/8 fl oz double cream
- grated rind of 2 limes
- 2 tbsp icing sugar

These dainty pies are delicious while warm. If you can find a passion fruit in the shops, cut it in half and scoop out the seeds over the whipped cream topping just before serving.

1. Preheat the oven to 180°C/350°F/Gas Mark 4. Lightly grease 2 x 12-section mini muffin tins.

2. Roughly chop the strawberries. Put them in a mixing bowl and stir in the cornflour, jam and lime rind.

3. Roll half the pastry out thinly on a lightly floured surface. Using a fluted cookie cutter, stamp out 24 circles, each 6 cm/2½ inches in diameter. Press these gently into the prepared tins, rerolling the trimmings as needed.

4. Brush the top edges of the pie cases with a little of the egg glaze, then spoon in the filling.

5. Roll the reserved pastry out thinly on a lightly floured surface. Stamp out 24 circles, each 5 cm/2 inches in diameter, rerolling the trimmings as needed. Use a cookie cutter to cut hearts from each circle, some tiny, some bigger. Use the rounds and bigger hearts as lids, pressing the edges together. Brush egg glaze over the pastry and sprinkle with caster sugar.

6. Bake in the preheated oven for 15 minutes, or until golden. Leave to cool in the tins for 10 minutes, then loosen with a round-bladed knife and transfer to a wire rack to cool. Whip the cream until it forms soft swirls, then fold in half the lime rind and all the icing sugar. Sprinkle with the rest of the lime rind. Serve spoonfuls of the cream with the pies.

Deep South cherry pies

Makes: 24 mini muffin sized pies
Prep: 30 minutes
Cook: 15 minutes

- a little butter, for greasing
- 350 g/12 oz cherries, stoned and halved, plus extra to decorate
- 2 tsp cornflour
- 3 tbsp caster sugar
- 1 tsp vanilla extract
- ½ tsp ground cinnamon
- 450 g/1 lb Sweet Shortcrust Pastry (see page 8) or ready-made sweet shortcrust pastry, chilled
- a little plain flour, for dusting
- 1 egg yolk mixed with 1 tbsp water, to glaze
- 2 tbsp caster sugar mixed with a large pinch ground cinnamon, for sprinkling

These are sure to evoke happy memories of childhood. They're delicious served still hot from the oven with a drizzle of custard or spoonful of vanilla ice cream.

1. Preheat the oven to 180°C/350°F/Gas Mark 4. Lightly grease 2 x 12-section mini muffin tins.

2. Put the stoned cherries in a mixing bowl and stir in the cornflour, sugar, vanilla extract and cinnamon.

3. Roll two-thirds of the pastry out thinly on a lightly floured surface. Using a fluted cookie cutter, stamp out 24 circles, each 6 cm/2½ inches in diameter. Press these into the prepared tins, rerolling the trimmings as needed.

4. Brush the top edges of the pie cases with a little of the egg glaze, then spoon in the filling.

5. Roll the reserved pastry out thinly on a lightly floured surface. Stamp out 24 circles, each 5 cm/2 inches in diameter, rerolling the trimmings as needed. Arrange these on top of the pies, pressing the edges together to seal. Brush over some egg glaze. Use a cookie cutter to cut tiny hearts and flowers from the remaining pastry and arrange these on the lids. Brush egg glaze over the decorations.

6. Bake in the preheated oven for 15 minutes, or until golden. Leave to cool in the tins for 10 minutes, then loosen with a round-bladed knife and transfer to a wire rack to cool. Serve warm or cold, sprinkled with the cinnamon mixture, on a plate decorated with extra cherries.

Peach and chocolate meringue pies

Makes: 6 muffin sized pies
Prep: 40 minutes
Cook: 22–25 minutes

What is there not to like? Crisp hazelnut pastry with a slightly tart peach filling that contrasts with a soft cloud of sweet meringue swirled with melted dark chocolate. You don't need to add anything, not even cream.

- 225 g/8 oz All Butter Hazelnut Pastry (see page 9) or ready-made sweet shortcrust pastry, chilled
- a little plain flour, for dusting
- 25 g/1 oz butter, plus extra for greasing
- 2 peaches, peeled if liked, halved, stoned and diced
- 50 g/1 3/4 oz dark chocolate, roughly chopped
- 2 egg whites
- 55 g/2 oz caster sugar

1. Lightly grease a 6-section muffin tin. Roll the pastry out thinly on a lightly floured surface. Using a plain cookie cutter, stamp out 6 circles each 10 cm/4 inches in diameter. Press these gently into the prepared tin, rerolling the trimmings as needed. Prick the base of each pie with a fork, then chill in the fridge for 15 minutes. Preheat the oven to 190°C/375°F/Gas Mark 5.

2. Line the pastry cases with squares of crumpled baking paper and baking beans (see page 6). Bake in the preheated oven for 10 minutes. Remove the paper and beans and cook the pastry cases for 2–3 minutes more, or until the base of the pastry is crisp and dry.

3. Meanwhile, melt the butter in a small frying pan or saucepan, add the peaches and cook gently for 5 minutes, stirring occasionally, until softened. Spoon the peaches into the pastry cases.

4. Put the chocolate in a heatproof bowl, set over a saucepan of gently simmering water and heat until melted. Whisk the egg whites in a large clean mixing bowl until you have stiff, moist-looking peaks, then gradually whisk in the sugar a teaspoon at a time for another 1–2 minutes, or until the meringue is very thick and glossy. Fold the melted chocolate into the meringue with just a couple of swirls of the spoon for a marbled effect. Spoon into the pies.

5. Bake in the preheated oven for 5–7 minutes, or until the meringue peaks are golden and just cooked through. Leave to cool in the tin for 10 minutes, then loosen with a round-bladed knife and transfer to a wire rack to cool. Serve warm.

Brandy apple pies

Makes: 24 mini muffin sized pies
Prep: 35 minutes
Cook: 20–25 minutes

These dainty little high-topped pies have been personalized by adding an initial made from a tiny rope of pastry for each of your dinner guests; if you have a set of little alphabet cutters then you may prefer to use these. If you wish, cook these pies in advance and freeze when cool, then warm through when needed.

- 450 g/1 lb cooking apples, quartered, cored, peeled and diced
- 25 g/1 oz butter, plus extra for greasing
- 55 g/2 oz caster sugar, plus extra for sprinkling
- 55 g/2 oz sultanas or raisins
- grated rind of 1 lemon
- 3 tbsp Bourbon or brandy
- 1 quantity All Butter Pastry (see page 9) or ready-made sweet shortcrust pastry, chilled
- a little plain flour, for dusting
- a little milk, to glaze
- whipped cream, to serve

1. Preheat the oven to 180°C/350°F/Gas Mark 4. Lightly grease 2 x 12-section mini muffin tins.

2. Put the apples in a medium saucepan with the butter, sugar, sultanas and lemon rind. Cook, uncovered, over a gentle heat, stirring from time to time, for 8–10 minutes, or until the apples have softened but still hold their shape. Add the Bourbon and cook until just bubbling. Keeping it over the heat, flame with a taper or long match, stand well back and cook for a minute or so, until the flame subsides. Leave the mixture to cool.

3. Roll half the pastry out thinly on a lightly floured surface. Using a fluted cookie cutter, stamp out 24 circles, each 6 cm/2½ inches in diameter. Press these gently into the prepared tins, rerolling the trimmings as needed.

4. Brush the top edges of the pie cases with milk, then spoon in the filling, doming it up high in the centre.

5. Roll the reserved pastry out thinly on a lightly floured surface. Stamp out 24 circles, the same size as before, rerolling the trimmings as needed. Arrange these on top of the pies, pressing the edges together well to seal. Brush milk over the pastry.

6. Shape tiny ropes from the remaining pastry into the initials of your dinner guests or family. Press these onto the pie tops, brush with a little extra milk and sprinkle with sugar.

7. Bake in the preheated oven for 15 minutes, or until golden. Leave to cool in the tins for 10 minutes, then loosen with a round-bladed knife and transfer to a wire rack to cool. Serve warm or cold, sprinkled with a little extra sugar, with spoonfuls of whipped cream.

Hot spiced pumpkin pies

Makes: 24 mini muffin sized pies
Prep: 30 minutes
Cook: 30 minutes

- a little butter, for greasing
- 250 g/9 oz pumpkin (weighed after deseeding and peeling), diced small
- 4 tbsp semi-skimmed milk
- 2 eggs
- 3 tbsp runny honey
- 1 tsp ground ginger
- ¼ tsp ground mixed spice
- 325 g/11½ oz All Butter Pastry (see page 9) or ready-made sweet shortcrust pastry, chilled
- a little plain flour, for dusting
- a little milk, to glaze
- a little caster sugar, for sprinkling

These are always popular for Halloween. Serve them as they are or top with a spoonful of whipped cream flavoured with a little honey or maple syrup.

1. Preheat the oven to 190°C/375°F/Gas Mark 5. Lightly grease 2 x 12-section mini muffin tins.

2. Put the pumpkin in a steamer, cover and set over a pan of gently simmering water. Steam for 15 minutes, or until tender. Purée with the milk in a liquidizer or food processor until smooth. Cool slightly, then mix in the eggs, honey, ginger and mixed spice.

3. Roll the pastry out thinly on a lightly floured surface. Using a plain cookie cutter, stamp out 24 circles, each 6 cm/2½ inches in diameter. Press these gently into the tins, rerolling the trimmings as needed. Squeeze any remaining trimmings together and reserve.

4. Brush the top edges of the pie cases with milk, then spoon in the filling.

5. Roll the remaining pastry trimmings out thinly on a lightly floured surface. Use a sharp knife to cut tiny leaves and mark on veins. Brush these with milk, arrange them over each pie and sprinkle with a little sugar.

6. Bake in the preheated oven for 15 minutes, or until the leaves are golden and the filling is just set. Leave to cool in the tins for 10 minutes, then loosen with a round-bladed knife and transfer to a wire rack to cool. Serve warm or cold, sprinkled with a little extra sugar.

2

5

Christmas cranberry and orange pies

Makes: 12 mini muffin sized pies
Prep: 30 minutes
Cook: 30 minutes

Cranberries needn't be kept just for sauce to go with the turkey; try them gently poached with star anise for a fragrant filling in an orange-scented pie crust. The secret to cooking cranberries is not to add sugar at first, but instead when the skins have softened. For a festive accompaniment serve with whipped cream flavoured with orange liqueur.

- a little butter, for greasing
- 175 g/6 oz frozen cranberries
- 1 tbsp cornflour
- 3 tbsp freshly squeezed orange juice
- 2 star anise
- 55 g/2 oz caster sugar, plus extra for sprinkling
- 225 g/8 oz Orange Sweet Shortcrust Pastry (see pages 8–9) or ready-made sweet shortcrust pastry, chilled
- a little plain flour, for dusting
- a little milk, to glaze
- a little caster sugar, for sprinkling

1. Preheat the oven to 180°C/350°F/Gas Mark 4. Lightly grease a 12-section mini muffin tin.

2. Put the still-frozen cranberries in a medium saucepan with the cornflour and orange juice. Add the star anise and cook uncovered over a low heat, stirring from time to time, for 5 minutes, or until the cranberries have softened. Add the sugar and cook for 5 minutes more, then leave to cool.

3. Roll the pastry out thinly on a lightly floured surface. Using a fluted cookie cutter, stamp out 12 circles, each 6 cm/2½ inches in diameter. Press these gently into the prepared tin, rerolling the trimmings as needed. Squeeze any remaining trimmings together and reserve.

4. Brush the top edges of the pie cases with a little milk. Discard the star anise, then spoon in the filling.

5. Roll the remaining pastry out thinly on a lightly floured surface. Using a fluted pastry wheel, cut thin strips of pastry. Arrange these over each pie and brush with a little milk. Sprinkle with a little sugar. Bake in the preheated oven for 20 minutes, covering with foil after 10 minutes if the tops are browning too quickly. Leave to cool in the tin for 10 minutes, then loosen with a round-bladed knife and transfer to a wire rack to cool. Serve warm or cold.

Shaker lemon pies

Makes: 24 mini muffin sized pies
Prep: 40 minutes
Cook: 55 minutes

These are traditionally made with thin-skinned Meyer lemons soaked for hours in sugar before baking, but as they are notoriously difficult to find, ordinary lemons have been used here instead. To get around the increased bitterness, two lemons are thinly sliced and poached in a sugar syrup, then mixed with extra grated lemon rind and juice for a tangy filling.

- 3½ medium lemons
- 250 g/9 oz caster sugar, plus extra for sprinkling
- 4 tbsp water
- 60 g/2¼ oz butter, plus extra for greasing
- 3 eggs
- 450 g/1 lb All Butter Pastry (see page 9) or ready-made sweet shortcrust pastry, chilled
- a little plain flour, for dusting
- egg white, to glaze

1. Lightly grease 2 x 12-section mini muffin tins. Thinly slice 2 of the lemons – you need 24 slices. Put them in a medium saucepan with 100 g/3½ oz the sugar and the water and stir. Cook uncovered over a low heat, stirring from time to time, for 30 minutes, or until the lemon slices are soft and translucent and only just beginning to lose their colour. Using a fork, scoop the lemon slices out of the saucepan, draining off the syrup, and put them on a plate; they will be used in step 5.

2. Preheat the oven to 180°C/350°F/Gas Mark 4. Grate the rind and squeeze the juice from the remaining lemons. Add them to the syrup with the butter and remaining sugar. Heat gently, uncovered, until the butter is just melted.

3. Meanwhile, beat the eggs in a small bowl. Remove the pan from the heat and strain the eggs through a sieve into it, stirring well. Return to the heat and cook very gently for 10 minutes, stirring frequently, or until the mixture has thickened and is jam-like. Increase the heat if needed but keep a watchful eye; too hot and the eggs will curdle. Leave to cool.

4. Roll half the pastry out thinly on a lightly floured surface. Using a fluted cookie cutter, stamp out 24 circles, each 6 cm/2½ inches in diameter. Press these gently into the prepared tins, rerolling trimmings as needed.

5. Brush the top edges of the cases with a little egg white, then spoon in the filling. Top each with a slice of the candied lemon made in step 1.

6. Roll the reserved pastry out thinly on a lightly floured surface. Stamp out 24 circles, each 5 cm/2 inches in diameter, rerolling the trimmings as needed. Press these on to the pie tops, pressing the edges together well.

7. Make 4 small cuts in the top of each pie, brush the pies with egg white and sprinkle with sugar. Bake in the preheated oven for 15 minutes, or until golden. Leave to cool in the tins for 10 minutes, then loosen with a round-bladed knife and transfer to a wire rack to cool. Serve warm or cold.

Lemon meringue pies

Makes: 12 muffin sized pies
Prep: 30 minutes
Cook: 18–22 minutes

This all-time classic is loved by everyone, with its sharp tangy lemon filling topped generously with piped or spooned meringue. These are made with a crumb crust.

- 100 g/3½ oz butter, plus extra for greasing
- 2 tbsp golden syrup
- 300 g/10½ oz graham crackers or digestive biscuits, crushed
- grated rind and juice of 3 lemons
- 200 g/7 oz caster sugar
- 40 g/1½ oz cornflour
- 3 eggs, separated

1. Preheat the oven to 180°C/350°F/Gas Mark 4. Lightly grease a 12-section muffin tin.

2. Put the butter and syrup in a small saucepan and heat until the butter has just melted. Take the pan off the heat, stir in the biscuit crumbs, then divide the mixture between the sections of the prepared tin. Press it firmly over the base and sides of the tin with the back of a teaspoon.

3. Line the cases with baking paper and baking beans, then bake them in the preheated oven for 8–10 minutes, or until slightly darker in colour. Leave to cool and harden in the tin for 10–15 minutes. Remove the paper and beans.

4. Put the lemon rind in a second, slightly larger saucepan. Make the juice up to 450 ml/16 fl oz with cold water, then add this liquid to the rind and bring just to the boil. In a mixing bowl, stir 85 g/3 oz sugar, the cornflour and egg yolks together until a thick paste has formed, then gradually stir in the boiling lemon juice until smooth.

5. Pour the liquid back into the saucepan and cook over a medium heat, stirring constantly, for a few minutes, until it is very thick and smooth. Spoon the filling into the crumb cases.

6. For the topping, whisk the egg whites in a large clean mixing bowl until you have stiff peaks, then gradually whisk in the remaining sugar a teaspoon at a time for another 1–2 minutes, or until the meringue is very thick and glossy. Spoon or pipe the meringue on top of the pies.

7. Bake in the preheated oven for 10–12 minutes, or until the meringue peaks are golden and just cooked through. Leave to cool and firm up in the tin, then loosen with a round-bladed knife and transfer to a plate.

S'more pies

Makes: 12 mini muffin sized pies
Prep: 20 minutes
Cook: 9–10 minutes

This summer camp favourite gets the grown-up treatment. Mini crumb cases flavoured with peanut butter, then filled with a rich dark chocolate cream and piled high with mini marshmallows. Great with cups of strong coffee or hot chocolate at the end of a barbecue.

- 40 g/1½ oz butter, plus extra for greasing
- 1 tbsp crunchy peanut butter
- 85 g/3 oz graham crackers or Rich Tea biscuits, crushed
- 100 g/3½ oz plain chocolate, roughly chopped
- 1 tbsp icing sugar
- 6 tbsp double cream
- 40 g/1½ oz mini marshmallows

1. Preheat the oven to 180°C/350°F/Gas Mark 4. Lightly grease a 12-section mini muffin tin.

2. Put the butter in a small saucepan. Gently heat, uncovered, until it has melted. Take the saucepan off the heat and stir in the peanut butter, then the biscuit crumbs. Divide between the sections of the prepared tin. Press it firmly over the base and sides of the tin with the back of a teaspoon.

3. Bake in the preheated oven for 6 minutes, or until slightly darker in colour. Reshape the centre if needed with the back of a spoon. Leave to cool and harden in the tin for 10–15 minutes.

4. Meanwhile, put the chocolate in a heatproof bowl, set the bowl over a saucepan of gently simmering water and heat until melted. Add the sugar and gradually stir in the cream until smooth. Preheat the grill to medium.

5. Spoon the filling into the cases. Sprinkle the mini marshmallows over the top and press them lightly into the chocolate so they don't roll off.

6. Grill for 3–4 minutes, or until the marshmallows have softened and are just beginning to colour. Leave to cool in the tin for 30 minutes, then loosen with a round-bladed knife and carefully lift out of the tin. Serve.

2

4

5

Tiny Tartlets

Blueberry tarts

Makes: 24 mini muffin sized pies
Prep: 25 minutes
Cook: 17–18 minutes

300 g/10½ oz blueberries

2 tsp cornflour

55 g/2 oz caster sugar

4 tsp water

55 g/2 oz plain flour, plus extra for dusting

grated rind of 1 lemon

40 g/1½ oz butter, diced, plus extra for greasing

325 g/11½ oz All Butter Pastry (see page 9) or ready-made sweet shortcrust pastry, chilled

Crisp, dainty pies with a moist blueberry filling and a buttery crumble top. Serve while still warm, with good vanilla ice cream.

1. Preheat the oven to 190°C/375°F/Gas Mark 5. Lightly grease 2 x 12-section mini muffin tins.

2. Put half the blueberries in a small saucepan with the cornflour, half the caster sugar and the water. Cook, uncovered, over a medium heat, stirring constantly, for 2–3 minutes, or until the juices begin to run and the sauce thickens. Take the pan off the heat and add the remaining blueberries.

3. For the streusel, put the flour, lemon rind, butter and remaining sugar in a medium mixing bowl. Toss together, then lift the mixture and rub it through your fingers and thumbs until it looks like fine breadcrumbs.

4. Roll the pastry out thinly on a lightly floured surface. Using a fluted cookie cutter, stamp out 24 circles each 6 cm/2½ inches in diameter. Press these into the prepared tins, rerolling trimmings as needed. Spoon the blueberry filling into the cases, then sprinkle the tops of the tarts with the streusel mixture.

5. Bake in the preheated oven for 15 minutes, or until the topping is pale gold. Leave to cool in the tins for 10 minutes, then loosen with a round-bladed knife and transfer to a wire rack to cool. Serve warm or cold.

2

3

4

Orchard tarts

Makes: 6 muffin sized pies
Prep: 45 minutes
Cook: 32–33 minutes

Apple pies with a twist; they are sprinkled with homemade granola (a mix of oats, seeds and nuts). Mix and match the topping ingredients to suit your larder; try barley flakes, flaked almonds, chopped macadamia nuts, golden linseeds or pumpkin seeds.

- a little butter, for greasing
- 225 g/8 oz All Butter Pastry (see page 9) or ready-made sweet shortcrust pastry, chilled
- a little plain flour, for dusting
- 1 pear, about 150 g/5½ oz, quartered, cored, peeled and diced
- 1 cooking apple, about 150 g/5½ oz, quartered, cored, peeled and diced
- 3 ripe red plums, halved, stoned and diced
- 25 g/1 oz caster sugar
- 1 tbsp water
- 1 tbsp sunflower oil
- 1 tbsp runny honey
- 4 tbsp porridge oats
- 1 tbsp sesame seeds
- 2 tbsp sunflower seeds
- 2 tbsp pumpkin seeds
- 2 tbsp hazelnuts, roughly chopped

1. Lightly grease a 6-section muffin tin. Roll the pastry out thinly on a lightly floured surface. Using a plain cookie cutter, stamp out 6 circles each 10 cm/4 inches in diameter. Press these gently into the prepared tin, rerolling the trimmings as needed. Prick the base of each with a fork, then chill in the fridge for 15 minutes. Preheat the oven to 190°C/375°F/Gas Mark 5.

2. Line the pastry cases with squares of crumpled baking paper and baking beans (see page 6). Bake in the preheated oven for 10 minutes. Remove the paper and beans and cook the cases for 2–3 minutes more, or until the base of the pastry is crisp and dry. Turn the oven down to 180°C/350°F/Gas Mark 4.

3. Put all the fruit, sugar and water in a medium saucepan. Cover and cook over a gentle heat, stirring, for 5 minutes, or until the fruit has just softened. Meanwhile, for the granola, warm the oil and honey in a frying pan. Stir in the oats, seeds and hazelnuts and set aside. Spoon the fruit into the cases, then sprinkle the granola on top.

4. Bake in the preheated oven for 20 minutes, covering with foil after 10 minutes if the granola is browning too quickly. Leave to cool in the tin for 10 minutes, then loosen with a round-bladed knife and transfer to a wire rack to cool. Serve warm.

Caramelized apple tarts

Makes: 12 muffin sized pies
Prep: 45 minutes
Cook: 32–36 minutes

These French-inspired tarts are filled with a tangy apple and lemon custard, then topped with wafer-thin sliced apples and glazed with a little icing sugar. They can be tricky to remove from the tin as the sugar glaze makes them sticky, so do take extra care.

- 450 g/1 lb Sweet Shortcrust Pastry (see page 8) or ready-made sweet shortcrust pastry, chilled
- a little plain flour, for dusting
- 5 Granny Smith apples, quartered, cored and peeled
- 85 g/3 oz caster sugar
- finely grated rind and juice of 1 lemon
- 2 eggs
- 15 g/½ oz butter, plus extra for greasing
- 3 tbsp icing sugar, sifted

1. Lightly grease a 12-section muffin tin. Roll the pastry out thinly on a lightly floured surface. Using a plain cookie cutter, stamp out 12 circles, each 10 cm/4 inches in diameter. Press these gently into the prepared tin, rerolling the trimmings as needed. Prick the base of each with a fork, then chill in the fridge for 15 minutes. Preheat the oven to 190°C/375°F/Gas Mark 5.

2. Line the pastry cases with squares of crumpled baking paper and baking beans (see page 6). Bake in the preheated oven for 10 minutes. Remove the paper and beans and cook the cases for 2–3 minutes more, or until the base of the pastry is crisp and dry. Turn the oven down to 180°C/350°F/Gas Mark 4.

3. Roughly grate 8 of the apple quarters into a mixing bowl. Add two-thirds of the caster sugar, all the lemon rind and juice and the eggs and whisk together. Spoon the filling into the cases.

4. Thinly slice the remaining apples and arrange them overlapping on top of the pies. Sprinkle with the remaining caster sugar and then dot the pies with the butter.

5. Bake in the preheated oven for 20–25 minutes, or until the filling is set and the sliced apples are browned around the edges.

6. Dust with the icing sugar and return the pies to the oven for 5 minutes, or until the sugar has caramelized. Leave to cool in the tin for 15 minutes, then loosen with a round-bladed knife and transfer to a wire rack to cool. Serve warm or cold.

Mississippi mud pies

Makes: 6 muffin sized pies
Prep: 30 minutes
Cook: 12–13 minutes

- a little butter, for greasing
- 225 g/8 oz Chocolate or Hazelnut Sweet Shortcrust Pastry (see pages 8–9) or ready-made sweet shortcrust pastry, chilled
- a little plain flour, for dusting
- 100 g/3½ oz plain chocolate, roughly chopped
- 4 tbsp icing sugar
- 125 ml/4 fl oz semi-skimmed milk
- 1 egg
- 225 ml/8 fl oz double cream
- 1 tsp vanilla extract
- white and dark chocolate curls, to decorate

A dark, rich, almost truffle-like chocolate layer encased in an even darker crisp chocolate pastry, then topped with soft swirls of Chantilly cream.

1. Lightly grease a 6-section muffin tin. Roll the pastry out thinly on a lightly floured surface. Using a plain cookie cutter, stamp out 6 circles each 10 cm/4 inches in diameter. Press these gently into the prepared tin, rerolling the trimmings as needed. Prick the base of each with a fork, then chill in the fridge for 15 minutes. Preheat the oven to 190°C/375°F/Gas Mark 5.

2. Line the pastry cases with squares of crumpled baking paper and baking beans (see page 6). Bake in the preheated oven for 10 minutes. Remove the paper and beans and cook the cases for 2–3 minutes more, or until the base of the pastry is crisp and dry.

3. Meanwhile, put the plain chocolate in a heatproof bowl, set the bowl over a saucepan of gently simmering water and heat until melted. Beat 2 tablespoons of sugar, the milk and egg together in a jug. Take the bowl of chocolate off the heat and gradually stir in the milk mixture until smooth. Pour the filling into the cases and leave to cool. Transfer the pies to the fridge for 2 hours, or until the filling has set.

4. Whip the cream with the remaining icing sugar and the vanilla until it forms soft folds. Loosen the pastry cases with a round-bladed knife and lift them onto a plate. Spoon the cream over the top and decorate with the chocolate curls.

2

3

Chocolate and pecan tarts

Makes: 24 mini muffin sized pies
Prep: 25 minutes
Cook: 20 minutes

These pies freeze well packed into a plastic box. Once defrosted, add a dusting of icing sugar and a drizzle of melted chocolate before serving. Alternatively, warm them in the oven and serve with whipped cream flavoured with ground cinnamon or Greek yogurt and honey.

- 115 g/4 oz golden syrup
- 70 g/2½ oz light muscovado sugar
- 25 g/1 oz butter, plus extra for greasing
- 50 g/1¾ oz dark chocolate, roughly chopped
- 325 g/11½ oz All Butter Cinnamon Pastry (see page 9) or ready-made sweet shortcrust pastry, chilled
- a little plain flour, for dusting
- 1 egg, beaten
- 1 egg yolk
- 85 g/3 oz pecan nuts
- 50 g/1¾ oz dark chocolate, roughly chopped, to decorate

1. Preheat the oven to 180°C/350°F/Gas Mark 4. Lightly grease a 2 x 12-section mini muffin tins.

2. Put the syrup, sugar and butter in a small saucepan. Heat gently, uncovered, stirring from time to time, until the butter has just melted. Add the chocolate and stir until it too has melted. Leave to cool slightly.

3. Roll the pastry out thinly on a lightly floured surface. Using a fluted cookie cutter, stamp out 24 circles each 6 cm/2½ inches in diameter. Press these gently into the prepared tins, rerolling the trimmings as needed.

4. Stir the egg and egg yolk into the cooled chocolate mixture until smooth, then spoon this filling into the cases. Decorate the top of each pie with 2 pecan nuts.

5. Bake in the preheated oven for 20 minutes, or until the filling has set, and covering with foil after 10 minutes if the nuts are browning too quickly. Leave to cool in the tins for 10 minutes, then loosen with a round-bladed knife and transfer to a wire rack to cool.

6. For the decoration, put the chocolate in a heatproof bowl, set the bowl over a saucepan of gently simmering water and heat until melted. Dust the tops of the pies with a little sifted icing sugar. Spoon the chocolate into a paper piping bag, snip off the tip and pipe zigzag lines of melted chocolate over the pies, or drizzle the chocolate from a teaspoon. Leave the pies to set for 10 minutes, then arrange on a serving plate.

Pistachio and almond tarts

Makes: 12 mini muffin sized pies
Prep: 20 minutes
Cook: 15 minutes

- 225 g/8 oz Sweet Shortcrust Pastry (see page 8) or ready-made sweet shortcrust pastry, chilled
- a little plain flour, for dusting
- 50 g/1¾ oz butter, softened, plus extra for greasing
- 50 g/1¾ oz caster sugar
- 1 egg yolk
- 50 g/1¾ oz ground almonds
- a few drops of almond extract or orange flower water
- 1½ tbsp flaked almonds
- 1 tbsp pistachio nuts, thinly sliced
- a little icing sugar, sifted, to decorate

A true French frangipane is made with just almonds, but a mixture of pretty green-tinged sliced pistachios and ground and flaked almonds makes for a luxurious mini pie.

1. Lightly grease a 12-section mini muffin tin. Preheat the oven to 180°C/350°F/Gas Mark 4.

2. Roll the pastry out thinly on a lightly floured surface. Using a fluted cookie cutter, stamp out 12 circles each 6 cm/2½ inches in diameter. Press these gently into the prepared tin, rerolling the trimmings as needed.

3. Meanwhile, put the butter and caster sugar in a mixing bowl and beat together until light and fluffy. Beat in the egg yolk, then the ground almonds. Flavour with a little almond essence or orange flower water.

4. Spoon the frangipane into the pastry cases.

5. Sprinkle the flaked almonds and sliced pistachios over the top and press them lightly into the filling.

6. Bake in the preheated oven for 15 minutes, or until the almonds are golden. Leave to cool in the tin for 10 minutes, then loosen with a round-bladed knife and transfer to a wire rack to cool. Serve warm or cold, dusted with sifted icing sugar.

Coffee tarts

Makes: 12 muffin sized pies
Prep: 40 minutes
Cook: 27–33 minutes

Dark, rich and not overly sweet. Bite through a crisp buttery pie case to a coffee and dark chocolate custard topped with whipped cream flavoured with coffee cream liqueur. Delicious served with a cup of strong black coffee.

- a little butter, for greasing
- 450 g/1 lb All Butter Pastry (see page 9) or ready-made sweet shortcrust pastry, chilled
- a little plain flour, for dusting
- 225 ml/8 fl oz semi-skimmed milk
- 115 g/4 oz plain chocolate, roughly chopped
- 2 tsp instant coffee powder or granules
- 2 tbsp caster sugar
- 2 eggs
- 2 egg yolks

DECORATION

- 200 ml/7 fl oz double cream
- 2 tbsp icing sugar
- 2 tbsp coffee cream liqueur
- 1½ tsp instant coffee dissolved in 1 tsp boiling water
- white chocolate curls, to decorate
- a dusting of cocoa, sifted, to decorate

1. Lightly grease a 12-section muffin tin. Roll the pastry out thinly on a lightly floured surface. Using a plain cookie cutter, stamp out 12 circles each 10 cm/4 inches in diameter. Press these gently into the prepared tin, rerolling the trimmings as needed. Prick the base of each with a fork, then chill for 15 minutes. Preheat the oven to 190°C/375°F/Gas Mark 5.

2. Line the pastry cases with squares of crumpled baking paper and baking beans (see page 6). Bake in the preheated oven for 10 minutes. Remove the paper and beans and cook the cases for 2–3 minutes more, or until the base of the pastry is crisp. Turn the oven down to 160°C/325°F/Gas Mark 3. Meanwhile, bring the milk just to the boil in a small saucepan. Add the chocolate, coffee and caster sugar and leave to stand, off the heat, until the chocolate has melted.

3. Beat the eggs and yolks in a mixing bowl, then gradually whisk in the warm milk mixture until smooth. Pour the custard into the pastry cases.

4. Bake in the preheated oven for 15–20 minutes, or until just set. Leave to cool in the tin for 10 minutes, then loosen with a round-bladed knife and transfer to a wire rack. Whip the cream in a bowl until it forms soft swirls. Add the sugar, then whisk in the liqueur and coffee until thick. Spoon over the pies, then decorate with white chocolate curls and a dusting of cocoa.

2

4

Creamy Classics

Cherry cream pies

Makes: 12 muffin sized pies
Prep: 30 minutes
Cook: 25-30 minutes

These light cheese pies are perfect for a special summer picnic, although you may need to pack them with a little crumpled foil or kitchen roll to cushion any knocks. Serve with a spoonful of whipped cream flavoured with a little sugar and vanilla.

- a little butter, for greasing
- 300 g/10½ oz mascarpone cheese
- 2 tsp plain flour, plus extra for dusting
- 85 g/3 oz caster sugar, plus extra for sprinkling
- 2 eggs
- 6 tbsp natural yogurt
- 1 tsp vanilla extract
- 450 g/1 lb All Butter Pastry (see page 9) or ready-made sweet shortcrust pastry, chilled
- a little milk, to glaze
- 36 fresh or canned cherries, stoned and drained well

1. Lightly grease a 12-section muffin tin. Preheat the oven to 180°C/350°F/ Gas Mark 4.

2. Spoon the mascarpone cheese into a mixing bowl and add the flour, sugar, eggs, yogurt and vanilla. Beat with a wooden spoon or electric hand-held whisk until just mixed.

3. Roll the pastry out thinly on a lightly floured surface. Using a plain cookie cutter, stamp out 12 circles each 10 cm/4 inches in diameter. Press these gently into the prepared tin, rerolling the trimmings as needed and reserving any remaining pastry. Brush the top edges of the pie cases with a little of the milk glaze and spoon in the filling. Add 3 cherries to each pie.

4. Roll the reserved pastry out thinly on a lightly floured surface. Cut strips about 1-cm/½-inch wide. Arrange 4 strips over each pie to make a lattice, pressing the edges together well to seal, then brush milk over the pastry and sprinkle with a little sugar.

5. Bake in the preheated oven for 25–30 minutes, or until the lattice is golden and the filling is just set. Leave to cool in the tin for 10 minutes, then loosen with a round-bladed knife and transfer to a wire rack to cool. Serve at room temperature.

3

4

Key lime pies

Makes: 24 mini muffin sized pies
Prep: 15 minutes
Cook: 6–8 minutes

- 4 tbsp golden syrup
- 70 g/2½ oz butter, plus extra for greasing
- 175 g/6 oz graham crackers or digestive biscuits, crushed
- 150 ml/5 fl oz double cream
- grated rind of 2 limes
- 200 g/7 oz canned sweetened condensed milk
- 4 tbsp freshly squeezed limes (about 2 limes)
- extra lime zest, to decorate

These super-speedy mini pies are filled with a luscious no-bake citrusy cream sweetened with condensed milk. They're great to make with kids.

1. Preheat the oven to 180°C/350°F/Gas Mark 4. Lightly grease 2 x 12-section mini muffin tins.

2. Put the syrup and butter in a small saucepan. Heat gently, uncovered, stirring, until the butter has just melted. Take the saucepan off the heat and stir in the biscuit crumbs. Divide the mixture between the sections of the prepared tins. Press it firmly over the base and sides of the tins with the back of a teaspoon.

3. Bake in the preheated oven for 6 minutes, or until slightly darker in colour. Reshape the centre if needed with the back of a spoon. Leave to cool and harden in the tins for 10–15 minutes.

4. Meanwhile, pour the cream into a bowl, add the lime rind and whisk until it is beginning to thicken. Gradually whisk in the condensed milk, then the lime juice, whisking for a few minutes more until it has thickened.

5. Pipe or spoon the lime cream into the cases. Chill for 30 minutes, or longer if you have time. Loosen the pies with a round-bladed knife and lift them carefully out of the tins. Decorate with lime zest curls.

Lemon and blueberry cheese pies

Makes: 12 muffin sized pies
Prep: 30 minutes
Cook: 23–30 minutes

Portions of cheesecake can be a struggle to wade through; not so with these morish individual pies. A tangy lemon cheesecake is held in a crisp chocolate crumb crust, then topped with slightly sharp soured cream and a blueberry compote. Depending on how many guests you have, or how big their appetites are, any leftover cheese pies can be frozen by wrapping each one in clingfilm and freezing the blueberry topping in a plastic container.

- 2 tbsp golden syrup
- 100 g/3½ oz butter, plus extra for greasing
- 300 g/10½ oz milk chocolate digestives or graham crackers, crushed
- 400 g/14 oz full-fat cream cheese
- 150 g/5½ oz caster sugar
- 150 ml/5 fl oz double cream
- 2 eggs
- grated rind and juice of 1 lemon
- 400 g/14 oz blueberries
- 2 tsp cornflour
- 4 tbsp water
- 250 ml/9 fl oz crème fraîche

1. Preheat the oven to 180°C/350°F/Gas Mark 4. Lightly grease a 12-section muffin tin.

2. Put the syrup and butter in a small saucepan. Heat gently, uncovered, stirring, until the butter has just melted. Take the saucepan off the heat and stir in the biscuit crumbs. Divide the mixture between the sections of the prepared tin. Press it firmly over the base and sides of the tin using the back of a teaspoon.

3. Line the cases with baking paper and baking beans, then bake them in the preheated oven for 8–10 minutes, or until slightly darker in colour. Leave to cool and harden in the tin for 10–15 minutes. Remove the paper and beans. Turn the oven down to 150°F/300°F/Gas Mark 2.

4. Put the cream cheese into a mixing bowl. Add 115 g/4 oz of the sugar and beat together briefly with an electric handheld whisk. Gradually beat in the cream and then the eggs until smooth. Add the lemon rind, then stir in half the juice. Spoon the filling into the crumb cases.

5. Bake in the preheated oven for 15–20 minutes, or until the filling is just set with a slight wobble to the centre. Turn the oven off, open the door slightly and leave the pies to cool in the oven.

6. For the topping, put half the blueberries in a medium saucepan. Add the cornflour, remaining sugar and remaining lemon juice, then stir in the water. Cook over a low heat until the juice begins to run from the blueberries, then increase the heat and cook until the sauce has thickened. Add the remaining blueberries and cook for 2 minutes more. Take off the heat and leave to cool.

7. Loosen the pies with a round-bladed knife and transfer to a plate. Chill in the fridge for several hours. When ready to serve, top each with a spoonful of crème fraîche and a generous spoonful of the blueberries.

Christmas candied orange and meringue pies

Makes: 12 mini muffin sized pies
Prep: 35 minutes
Cook: 35 minutes

Cooking the clementine peel and flesh in a sugar syrup until soft and candied adds an almost marmalade-like sweet tangy flavour to these brown sugar meringue-topped pies.

- a little butter, for greasing
- 225 g/8 oz Sweet Shortcrust Pastry (see page 8) or ready-made sweet shortcrust pastry, chilled
- a little plain flour, for dusting
- 2 clementines or 1 small thin-skinned orange
- 85 g/3 oz caster sugar
- 150 ml/5 fl oz water
- 150 g/5½ oz ready-to-eat dried apricots, diced
- 2 egg whites
- 25 g/1 oz soft light brown sugar
- orange rind curls, to decorate

1. Lightly grease a 12-section mini muffin tin. Preheat the oven to 180°C/350°F/Gas Mark 4.

2. Roll the pastry out thinly on a lightly floured surface. Using a fluted cookie cutter, stamp out 12 circles each 6 cm/2½ inches in diameter. Press these gently into the prepared tin, rerolling the trimmings as needed. Chill for 15 minutes.

3. Line the pastry cases with squares of crumpled baking paper and baking beans (see page 6). Bake in the preheated oven for 8 minutes. Remove the paper and beans and cook the cases for 2–3 minutes more, or until the base of the pastry is crisp and dry.

4. Meanwhile, peel the clementines and finely chop the rind. Separate the clementine segments, then roughly chop the flesh. Put the rind, two-thirds of the caster sugar and the water in a small saucepan, cover and simmer gently for 20 minutes. Add the flesh and the apricots and cook for 10 minutes more, or until soft and the water is driven off.

5. Spoon the orange filling into the pastry cases. Whisk the egg whites in a small clean mixing bowl until you have stiff, moist-looking peaks, then gradually whisk in the remaining caster sugar and the soft light brown sugar a teaspoon at a time for another 2 minutes, or until the meringue is very thick and glossy. Spoon or pipe the meringue onto the pies.

6. Bake in the preheated oven for 4–5 minutes, or until the meringue peaks are golden and just cooked through. Leave to cool in the tin for 10 minutes, then loosen with a round-bladed knife and transfer to a wire rack to cool. Serve warm, decorated with orange rind curls.

Maple cream pies with orange

Makes: 12 muffin sized pies
Prep: 45 minutes
Cook: 37–38 minutes

- a little butter, for greasing
- 450 g/1 lb All Butter Pastry (see page 9) or ready-made sweet shortcrust pastry, chilled
- a little plain flour, for dusting
- 225 ml/8 fl oz double cream
- 125 ml/4 fl oz maple syrup
- 2 eggs
- 2 egg yolks
- grated rind of 1 orange

TO SERVE

- 3 oranges, peeled and segmented
- 3 tbsp maple syrup

Delicately flavoured creamy custard pies with a hint of maple and orange rind. Delicious served at room temperature, with extra orange segments and a drizzle of maple syrup.

1. Lightly grease a 12-section muffin tin. Roll the pastry out thinly on a lightly floured surface. Using a fluted cookie cutter, stamp out 12 circles, each 10 cm/4 inches in diameter. Press these gently into the prepared tin, rerolling the trimmings as needed. Prick the base of each with a fork, then chill in the fridge for 15 minutes. Preheat the oven to 190°C/375°F/Gas Mark 5.

2. Line the pastry cases with squares of crumpled baking paper and baking beans (see page 6). Bake in the preheated oven for 10 minutes. Remove the paper and beans and cook the pastry cases for 2–3 minutes more, or until the base of the pastry is crisp and dry. Turn the oven down to 160°C/325°F/Gas Mark 3.

3. Whisk the cream, syrup, eggs, egg yolks and most of the orange rind together in a jug. Pour this filling into the pie cases.

4. Bake in the preheated oven for 25 minutes, or until the custard is set. Leave to cool in the tins for 10 minutes, then loosen with a round-bladed knife and transfer to a serving plate.

5. Serve topped with extra orange segments, a sprinkling of the remaining grated orange rind and a drizzle of maple syrup.

2

5

Honey, walnut and ricotta pies

Makes: 24 mini muffin sized pies
Prep: 45 minutes
Cook: 25 minutes

Made here with a crisp, rich, all butter pastry, these would also taste great with cinnamon shortcrust. The perfect pie for those who don't have a sweet tooth. Undecorated pies will keep in the fridge for two to three days.

- a little butter, for greasing
- a little olive oil, for greasing
- 325 g/11½ oz All Butter Pastry (see page 9) or ready-made sweet shortcrust pastry, chilled
- a little plain flour, for dusting
- 125 g/4½ oz walnut pieces
- 225 g/8 oz ricotta cheese
- 2 egg yolks
- 5 tbsp runny orange blossom honey
- a large pinch of ground cinnamon
- 115 g/4 oz granulated sugar
- 1 tbsp water
- 200 g/7 oz Greek yogurt, to serve

1. Lightly grease 2 x 12-section mini muffin tins and oil a baking tray. Preheat the oven to 180°C/350°F/Gas Mark 4.

2. Roll the pastry out thinly on a lightly floured surface. Using a fluted cookie cutter, stamp out 24 circles each 6 cm/2½ inches in diameter. Press these gently into the prepared tins, rerolling the trimmings as needed.

3. Lightly toast half the walnut pieces in a dry non-stick frying pan. Leave them to cool, then roughly chop them.

4. Lightly whisk the ricotta, egg yolks, 4 tablespoons of the honey and the cinnamon together in a mixing bowl until just mixed. Stir in the toasted walnuts. Spoon the filling into the cases.

5. Bake in the preheated oven for 20 minutes, or until the filling is golden brown. Leave in the tin for 10 minutes to cool.

6. Meanwhile, for the praline put the sugar, remaining 1 tablespoon of honey and the water into the frying pan and heat gently without stirring until the sugar has dissolved. Tilt the pan to mix any remaining grains of sugar into the syrup. Add the remaining walnuts and cook over a medium heat, again without stirring, for about 5 minutes, or until the syrup turns a rich golden brown. Keep a watchful eye on the syrup as it will suddenly begin to change colour, darkening first around the edges. Tilt the pan to mix if needed, then quickly pour the praline onto the prepared baking tray and leave to cool and harden.

7. Loosen the pies with a round-bladed knife and transfer them to a plate. Just before serving, top them with spoonfuls of yogurt. Loosen the praline from the baking tray with a knife, then break or cut it into thin shards and press pieces of it into the yogurt.

Coconut cream pies

Makes: 12 muffin sized pies
Prep: 40 minutes
Cook: 8–10 minutes

An all-American favourite made with a coconut confectioners' custard and topped with vanilla cream. Ginger fans could try a little chopped crystallised stem ginger in the cream instead of the vanilla flavouring.

- 2 tbsp golden syrup
- 100 g/3½ oz butter, plus extra for greasing
- 300 g/10½ oz gingersnap or digestive biscuits, crushed
- 85 g/3 oz unsweetened desiccated coconut
- 125 ml/4 fl oz boiling water
- 55 g/2 oz caster sugar
- 20 g/¾ oz cornflour
- 20 g/¾ oz plain flour
- 2 egg yolks
- 300 ml/10 fl oz milk
- grated rind of 1 lime
- 300 ml/10 fl oz double cream
- 1 tsp vanilla extract
- 2 tbsp icing sugar
- toasted coconut curls or desiccated coconut

1. Preheat the oven to 180°C/350°F/Gas Mark 4. Lightly grease a 12-section muffin tin.

2. Put the syrup and butter in a small saucepan. Heat gently, uncovered, stirring, until the butter has just melted. Take the saucepan off the heat and stir in the biscuit crumbs. Divide the mixture between the sections of the prepared tin. Press it firmly over the base and sides of the tin with the back of a teaspoon.

3. Line the cases with baking paper and baking beans, then bake them in the preheated oven for 8–10 minutes, or until slightly darker in colour. Leave to cool and harden in the tin for 10–15 minutes. Remove the paper and beans.

4. Put the coconut into a mixing bowl and pour over the boiling water. Leave to stand for 10 minutes. Put the sugar, cornflour, plain flour and egg yolks in a separate mixing bowl and beat together.

5. Pour the milk into a small saucepan, bring just to the boil, then gradually whisk it into the egg yolk mixture until smooth. Return the milk mixture to the saucepan and cook over a medium heat, whisking, until thick. The sauce will suddenly thicken, and as it does you may find it easier to turn the heat right down to low so that you can whisk out any lumps quickly. Stir in the soaked coconut and the lime rind, cover the surface with wetted baking paper and leave to cool.

6. Loosen the pie cases with a round-bladed knife and carefully lift out of the tin. Spoon in the coconut filling.

7. Whip the cream until it just forms soft swirls, then fold in the vanilla extract and sugar. Spoon this over the tops of the pies, then decorate with coconut curls or desiccated coconut.

Super Savouries

Steak and ale pies

Makes: 12 muffin sized pies
Prep: 30 minutes
Cook: 30–35 minutes

Adding a little dried English mustard to the pastry gives these pies a wonderful colour and flavour and complements their full-bodied filling. If you are short of time, ready-made shortcrust pastry will work just as well.

- 1 tbsp olive oil
- 15 g/½ oz salted butter, plus extra for greasing
- 500 g/1 lb 2 oz sirloin or rump steak, fat discarded and meat cut into 2.5-cm/1-inch cubes
- 2 shallots, finely chopped
- 150 g/5½ oz button mushrooms, sliced
- 1 bay leaf
- 1 tbsp plain flour, plus extra for dusting
- 225 ml/8 fl oz brown ale
- 125 ml/4 fl oz beef stock
- 1 tbsp tomato purée
- 1 quantity Mustard Shortcrust Pastry (see pages 8–9), or 650 g/1 lb 7 oz ready-made shortcrust pastry, chilled
- 1 egg yolk mixed with 1 tbsp water, to glaze
- salt flakes and pepper

1. Preheat the oven to 180°C/350°F/Gas Mark 4. Lightly grease a 12-section muffin tin.

2. To make the filling, heat the oil and butter in a frying pan over a medium heat. Add the steak, finely chopped shallots, mushrooms and bay and fry, stirring, until the steak is evenly browned and the shallots are golden brown.

3. Sprinkle the flour over the top, mix together, then add the brown ale, stock, tomato purée and a little salt and pepper. Simmer for 5 minutes, stirring from time to time, until the sauce has thickened. Leave to cool, then remove the bay.

4. Roll two-thirds of the pastry out thinly on a lightly floured surface. Using a plain cookie cutter, stamp out 12 circles each 10 cm/4 inches in diameter. Press these gently into the prepared muffin tin, rerolling the trimmings as needed.

5. Brush the top edges of the pie cases with a little of the egg glaze, then spoon in the filling.

6. Roll out the reserved pastry and any trimmings on a lightly floured surface. Using a plain cookie cutter, stamp out 12 circles each 7 cm/3 inches in diameter for the pie lids. Arrange these on top of the pies, pressing the edges together well with the tines of a fork to seal. Brush egg glaze over the pastry. Sprinkle with a little salt and pepper.

7. Bake in the preheated oven for 25 minutes, or until the pastry is golden. Leave to cool in the tins for 5 minutes, then loosen with a round-bladed knife and transfer to a wire rack.

Lamb and rosemary pasties

Makes: 12 mini pasties
Prep: 30 minutes
Cook: 37–38 minutes

- 2 tbsp olive oil
- 450 g/1 lb lean leg of lamb or lamb fillet, cut into 1 cm/½ inch cubes
- 200 g/7 oz potato, diced
- 6 spring onions, finely chopped
- 2 garlic cloves, finely chopped
- 150 g/5 oz cherry tomatoes, halved
- 1 quantity Herb Shortcrust Pastry (see pages 8–9), or 650 g/1 lb 7 oz ready-made shortcrust pastry, chilled
- a little plain flour, for dusting
- 1 egg yolk mixed with 1 tbsp water, to glaze
- salt flakes and pepper
- rosemary sprigs, to garnish

These rustic little hand-shaped pies are great for an informal weekend lunch while out working out in the garden.

1. Preheat the oven to 180°C/350°F/Gas Mark 4. Line a large baking sheet with non-stick baking paper.

2. Heat the oil in a frying pan over a medium heat. Add the lamb and potato and fry, stirring, for 10 minutes, or until the lamb is browned and the potato just tender. Add the spring onions, garlic, tomatoes and plenty of salt and pepper and cook for 2–3 minutes more, or until the tomatoes are just beginning to soften, then leave to cool.

3. Roll the pastry out thinly on a lightly floured surface. Using a plain cookie cutter, stamp out 12 circles each 12.5 cm/5 inches in diameter, rerolling the trimmings as needed.

4. Spoon the filling into the centre of each circle, then brush the edges of the pastry with a little of the egg glaze.

5. Fold the pastry over the filling to make half-moon-shaped pasties, pressing the edges together well to seal. Roll the edge, then mark with a knife. Transfer the pasties to the prepared baking sheet, brush them with egg and sprinkle with a some salt flakes and a few rosemary sprigs.

6. Bake in the preheated oven for 25 minutes, or until the pies are golden. Leave to cool on the baking sheet for 5 minutes, then serve hot or cold, sprinkled with flaked salt.

Chicken pot pies

Makes: 12 muffin sized pies
Prep: 30 minutes
Cook: 42 minutes

These dainty pies are ideal for a girlie lunch. If you are feeling extra hungry you may have room for two. If not the kids will be happy to devour any leftovers when they come back from school ravenous.

- 25 g/1 oz salted butter, plus extra for greasing
- 1 tbsp olive oil
- 500 g/1 lb 2 oz boneless, skinless chicken breasts, cut into 1 cm/½ inch cubes
- 1 leek, about 175 g/6 oz, thinly sliced, white and green slices kept separate
- 2 tbsp plain flour, plus extra for dusting
- 450 ml/16 fl oz chicken stock
- 4 tbsp Noilly Pratt or dry white wine
- 2 tbsp roughly chopped fresh tarragon
- 2 tbsp roughly chopped fresh parsley
- 1 tbsp chopped capers
- 1 quantity Savoury Shortcrust Pastry (see page 8) or 650 g/1 lb 7 oz ready-made plain shortcrust pastry, chilled
- 1 egg yolk mixed with 1 tbsp water, to glaze
- salt and pepper
- blanched asparagus, to serve

1. Preheat the oven to 180°C/350°F/Gas Mark 4. Lightly grease a 12-section muffin tin.

2. Heat the butter and oil in a frying pan over a medium heat. Add the chicken and white sliced leeks and fry, stirring, for 10 minutes, or until the chicken is golden brown and the leeks are softened.

3. Sprinkle the flour over the top, mix together, then add the stock, Noilly Pratt and a little salt and pepper. Simmer for 5 minutes, stirring from time to time, until the sauce has thickened and the chicken is cooked through. Add the green leek slices and cook for 2 minutes, or until the leeks are just soft. Sprinkle over the tarragon, parsley and capers and leave to cool.

4. Roll two-thirds of the pastry out thinly on a lightly floured surface. Using a plain cookie cutter, stamp out 12 circles each 10 cm/4 inches in diameter. Press these gently into the prepared muffin tin, rerolling the trimmings as needed.

5. Brush the top edges of the pie cases with a little of the egg glaze, then spoon in the filling.

6. Roll out the reserved pastry and any trimmings on a lightly floured surface. Using a plain cookie cutter, stamp out 12 circles each 7 cm/3 inches in diameter. Arrange these on top of the pies, pressing the edges together well to seal. Decorate the pastry edge by pressing it between the finger and thumb of your left hand and then pressing the edge with your right index finger or a small knife to make a scalloped pattern. Brush the pastry with egg glaze; add leaves cut out from rolled pastry trimmings using a sharp knife, then brush these with egg too.

7. Bake in the preheated oven for 25 minutes, or until golden brown. Leave to cool in the tin for 5 minutes, then loosen with a round-bladed knife and transfer to serving plates. Serve hot or cold with asparagus.

Turkey pies with cranberry and red onion relish

Makes: 12 muffin sized pies
Prep: 20 minutes
Cook: 33-34 minutes

- 300 g/10½ oz Savoury Shortcrust Pastry (see page 8) or ready-made shortcrust pastry, chilled
- a little plain flour, for dusting
- 1 egg yolk mixed with 1 tbsp water, to glaze
- 300 g/10½ oz minced turkey
- 4 spring onions, finely chopped
- 2 garlic cloves, finely chopped
- 4 stems fresh thyme, leaves torn from stems
- 1 tsp ground allspice
- 2 egg yolks
- salt and cayenne pepper

TO GARNISH

- 1 tbsp olive oil
- 1 red onion, thinly sliced
- 85 g/3 oz frozen cranberries
- 3 tbsp cranberry sauce
- 4 tbsp ruby Port or red wine

These mini pies make great snacks that the family can help themselves to from the fridge, as and when they get peckish.

1. Preheat the oven to 180°C/350°F/Gas Mark 4. Line a 12-section muffin tin with squares of non-stick baking paper.

2. Roll the pastry out thinly on a lightly floured surface. Using a plain cookie cutter, stamp out 12 circles each 12.5 cm/5 inches in diameter. Press these gently into the prepared muffin tin, so the pastry stands just above the top of the tin in soft pleats, rerolling the trimmings as needed.

3. Brush the top edges of the pie cases with a little of the egg glaze.

4. Put the turkey, onions, garlic and thyme leaves into a mixing bowl. Sprinkle over the allspice and a little salt and cayenne pepper, then stir in the egg yolks until well mixed. Spoon the filling into the pie cases and press the tops flat with the back of a teaspoon.

5. Bake in the preheated oven for 30 minutes, or until the pastry is golden and the filling is cooked through. Leave to cool in the tins for 5 minutes, then loosen with a round-bladed knife and transfer to a wire rack.

6. Meanwhile, for the garnish, heat the oil in a frying pan, add the red onion and cook until just beginning to soften. Add the remaining ingredients and cook for 3–4 minutes, or until the cranberries are soft. Spoon over the top of the baked pies and serve.

Salmon pies with dill gremolata

Makes: 12 muffin sized pies
Prep: 30 minutes
Cook: 15 minutes

Bite through a thin buttery filo case to a rich creamy sauce extravagantly filled with moist chunks of fresh salmon. Seafood fans may like to add prawns or flavour the sauce with dark crab meat and add the white crab meat towards the end of cooking.

- 40 g/1½ oz salted butter, plus extra for greasing
- 3 x 48-cm x 25-cm/19-inch x 10-inch sheets frozen filo pastry, defrosted

FILLING

- 2 salmon steaks, about 350 g/12 oz in total
- 300 ml/10 fl oz semi-skimmed milk
- 25 g/1 oz salted butter
- 6 spring onions, thinly sliced
- 25 g/1 oz plain flour
- 2 tbsp crème fraîche
- 2 tbsp Noilly Pratt, dry white wine or dry sherry
- 2 tbsp roughly chopped fresh dill
- grated rind of 1 lemon
- salt and pepper

1. Preheat the oven to 180°C/350°F/Gas Mark 4. Lightly grease a 12-section muffin tin. Put the butter into a small saucepan and heat until it has just melted.

2. Unfold 1 sheet of pastry, brush it with a little melted butter, then cut it into 8 pieces, each 12-cm/4½-inches square. Press 1 piece into a section of the prepared tin, then layer a second piece on top at right angles to the first. Continue in the remaining sections, with the remaining filo, until you have 12 x 2-layer cases. Roll the top edges down to make a pie crust.

3. Bake in the preheated oven for 5 minutes, or until golden and crisp, then lift the cases out of the tin and put them onto a plate.

4. Meanwhile, put the salmon in a medium saucepan, pour over the milk and season with a little salt and pepper. Cover and simmer gently for 10 minutes, or until the fish is just cooked. Lift the fish out of the milk, pour the milk into a jug and reserve, then wash and dry the pan.

5. Heat the butter in the pan until melted, then add the spring onions and fry for 2 minutes, or until just softened. Stir in the flour, cook 1 minute more, then gradually mix in the reserved milk plus the crème fraîche and Noilly Pratt and bring to the boil, stirring until thickened and smooth.

6. Flake the fish into chunky pieces, discarding any skin and bones. Add the flakes of fish to the sauce and reheat if needed. Spoon the hot filling into the pastry cases, then mix the dill and lemon rind together and sprinkle over the top.

Egg and sunblush tomato pies

Makes: 12 muffin sized pies
Prep: 30 minutes
Cook: 20 minutes

These deep-dish pies have a quiche-style filling flavoured with sunblush tomatoes and brie. They're perfect for family picnics or packing into work or school lunchboxes.

- a little butter, for greasing
- 450 g/1 lb Savoury Shortcrust Pastry (see page 8) or ready-made shortcrust pastry, chilled
- a little plain flour, for dusting
- 4 eggs
- 150 ml/5 fl oz milk
- 6 spring onions, finely chopped
- 2 tbsp roughly chopped fresh basil
- 175 g/6 oz brie, diced
- 100 g/3½ oz sunblush tomatoes, finely sliced
- salt and pepper

1. Preheat the oven to 180°C/350°F/Gas Mark 4. Lightly grease a 12-section muffin tin.

2. Roll the pastry out thinly on a lightly floured surface. Using a plain cookie cutter, stamp out 12 circles each 10 cm/4 inches in diameter. Press these gently into the prepared muffin tin, rerolling the pastry trimmings as needed.

3. Put the eggs, milk and a little salt and pepper together in a large jug and beat lightly with a fork. Mix in the onions and basil. Pour the filling into the pie cases, then sprinkle the brie and tomatoes on top.

4. Bake in the preheated oven for 20 minutes, or until the pastry is golden and the filling is set. Leave to cool in the tin for 10 minutes, then loosen with a round-bladed knife and transfer to a wire rack.

2

3

Mini Greek spinach and pine nut pies

Makes: 12 muffin sized pies
Prep: 20 minutes
Cook: 20–25 minutes

- 55 g/2 oz salted butter, plus extra for greasing
- 4 x 48-cm x 25-cm/19-inch x 10-inch sheets of frozen filo pastry, defrosted

FILLING

- 250 g/9 oz baby spinach leaves, rinsed with cold water and drained
- 1 tbsp olive oil
- 1 small onion, finely chopped
- 2 garlic cloves, finely chopped
- 100 g/3½ oz feta cheese, drained and grated
- 200 g/7 oz medium-fat soft cheese
- 2 eggs
- a little grated nutmeg
- salt and pepper
- 3 tbsp pine nuts, to garnish

These Greek-inspired pies are great to offer to visiting veggie friends, but be sure to check the cheese carries the vegetarian symbol.

1. Preheat the oven to 180°C/350°F/Gas Mark 4. Lightly grease a 12-section muffin tin.

2. To make the filling, preheat a frying pan over a medium heat. Add the spinach and stir fry for 2–3 minutes, or until just wilted. Scoop it out of the pan, add it to a large sieve and press out any remaining liquid. Heat the oil in the empty pan, add the onion and garlic and fry over a medium heat until softened.

3. Put the feta and soft cheese in a mixing bowl. Stir, then beat in the eggs one at a time and season with nutmeg, salt and pepper. Finely chop the spinach and stir this and the onion and garlic in too.

4. For the pastry cases, put the butter into a small saucepan and heat until it has just melted.

5. Unfold 1 sheet of pastry, brush it with a little melted butter, then cut it into 8 pieces, each 12 cm/4½ inches square. Press 1 piece into a section of the prepared tin, then layer a second piece on top at right angles to the first. Continue like this in the remaining sections, with 2 more sheets of filo, until you have 12 x 2-layer cases.

6. Divide the spinach filling between the pies. Fold the edges of the pastry over the filling. Tear strips from the remaining pastry sheet, crumple this over the top of the pies, brush with the remaining butter and sprinkle on the pine nuts.

7. Bake in the preheated oven for 20–25 minutes, or until the pastry is golden and pies have risen slightly. Check on the pies after 15 minutes and cover with foil if the nuts seem to be browning too quickly. Leave to cool in the tin for 10 minutes, then loosen with a round-bladed knife and transfer to a serving plate. Serve warm or cold.

Index

Mini Cakes

Mini Cakes

LOVE FOOD™

This edition published in 2012

LOVE FOOD is an imprint of Parragon Books Ltd

Parragon
Chartist House
15-17 Trim Street
Bath BA1 1HA, UK

Copyright © Parragon Books Ltd 2011

LOVE FOOD and the accompanying heart device is a registered trade mark of Parragon Books Ltd in Australia, the UK, USA, India and the EU.

www.parragon.com/lovefood

All rights reserved. No part of this publication may be reproduced, stored in a retrieval system or transmitted, in any form or by any means, electronic, mechanical, photocopying, recording or otherwise, without the prior permission of the copyright holder.

ISBN 978-1-4454-8746-5

Printed in China

Created and produced by Pene Parker and Becca Spry
Author and home economist: Joanna Farrow
Photographer: Noel Murphy

Notes for the Reader
This book uses both metric and imperial measurements. Follow the same units of measurement throughout; do not mix metric and imperial. All spoon measurements are level: teaspoons are assumed to be 5 ml, and tablespoons are assumed to be 15 ml. Unless otherwise stated, milk is assumed to be full fat, eggs and individual vegetables are medium, and pepper is freshly ground black pepper. Unless otherwise stated, all root vegetables should be washed and peeled prior to using.

Garnishes, decorations and serving suggestions are all optional and not necessarily included in the recipe ingredients or method.

The times given are an approximate guide only. Preparation times differ according to the techniques used by different people and the cooking times may also vary from those given. Optional ingredients, variations or serving suggestions have not been included in the time calculations.

Recipes using raw or very lightly cooked eggs should be avoided by infants, the elderly, pregnant women, convalescents and anyone suffering from an illness. Pregnant and breastfeeding women are advised to avoid eating peanuts and peanut products. Sufferers from nut allergies should be aware that some of the ready-made ingredients used in the recipes in this book may contain nuts. Always check the packaging before use.

Contents

Introduction

Tiny portions of our favourite treats are so much fun to bake and eat. They're in great demand, perhaps because they have the 'cute factor' that large portions don't, or because they're so easy to pop into our mouths. From tiny little fruit loaves to miniature wedding cakes, this book of bite-sized morsels offers something for every occasion.

Equipment

A minimal amount of baking equipment is needed to make the cakes in this book. What you don't have already is widely available from cake-decorating stores or via the internet.

Mini cupcake and muffin cases

Mini cupcake and muffin paper cases tend to vary considerably in size. The recipes in this book require paper cases with a base diameter of 3 cm/1¼ inches and 4 cm/1½ inches. Mini silicone cases are also available in a variety of colours, from subtle to bright. They're dishwasher-proof and reusable, and cakes are easy to remove from them by peeling away the cases. To bake, simply set silicone cases on a baking tray rather than in a muffin tray or cupcake tray. Neither silicone cases nor paper cases need greasing.

Mini cupcake and muffin tins

Paper cupcake cases and muffin cases must sit comfortably in the tin's sections, which should offer some support but not crease the paper cases up. Mini cupcake tins and mini muffin tins both have 12 or 24 sections; if using a 12-section tin you will need to bake two batches of cakes for some recipes in this book.

Mini loaf tins

Mini loaves can be made in a 12-section silicone loaf tray with sections measuring 7 x 5 cm/3 x 2 inches. Alternatively they can be made in individual metal tins, but these are usually slightly larger, so you won't make as many cakes as the recipe states and you will need a little extra cooking time. Silicone trays don't need lining, but line each metal tin with a wide strip of baking paper that goes over the base and up the long sides.

Mini sectioned cake tins

Both round and square sectioned cake tins measure 5 cm/2 inches in diameter per section and are usually bought in packs of 16, which fit onto a base for baking. Alternatively bake a large sponge cake and let it firm up for 24 hours, then cut out 5-cm/2-inch rounds or squares using a metal cutter as a guide.

Metal cookie cutters

Cookie cutters can be used to cut out shapes from sponge cakes such as the moons on page 60. Cutters are available in a variety of shapes and sizes and are sometimes sold seasonally, so it's worth collecting your favourite shapes when you see them.

Small square cake tins

An 18-cm/7-inch square cake tin is a useful size for baking sponges to cut into small cakes. Grease and line the base and sides of the tin before baking.

Baking techniques

Preparing tins
Use greaseproof paper or baking paper to line tins and melted butter or vegetable oil to grease them.

Lining square tins
Place the tin on baking paper, draw around the tin and cut out the paper just inside the lines. Cut a strip the depth of the tin and make a 1-cm/½-inch fold along one long edge. Grease the tin using a pastry brush and fit the strip around the sides so the folded strip sits on the base. Snip the folded edge at the corners. Press the paper square into the base and grease the paper.

Lining round sectioned tins
Grease the sections. Cut out circles of baking paper 1 cm/½ inch larger than the section diameters. Make 5 mm/¼ inch cuts at the sides of the circles and press them in sections so the snipped edges go up the sides.

Mixing muffins
Muffins are made by adding the wet ingredients to the dry ingredients. The flour is usually sifted first. Add the wet ingredients all in one go and fold everything together gently. As soon as they're combined but with specks of flour still visible, spoon the mixture into the cases. Over-mixing muffins can make them less light.

Filling cases
Unless otherwise stated, fill cupcake cases until they're almost full and the mixture is level with the top of the cases. For muffins the mixture can extend above the tops of the cases slightly to achieve the 'muffin top'.

How to tell if a cake is cooked
Cakes are usually slightly domed in the centre with a lightly browned surface. Gently touch the surface with your flattened fingers; it should feel just firm. Some cakes require a further test of pushing a skewer into the centre; if cooked the skewer will come out clean.

Decorating techniques

Applying frostings and creams

Take a little of the frosting from the bowl using a small palette knife. Spread the frosting gently over each cake to cover it in an even layer before refining the application with the flat edge of the knife to level the surface.

Colouring ready-to-roll icing and marzipan

Using a cocktail stick, dot a little food colouring onto the icing paste. If you want a delicate colour, use a tiny amount as a little goes a long way. Working on a surface dusted with icing sugar, knead in the colour.

Covering cakes with ready-to-roll icing

Take the required amount of icing and roll it out thinly on a surface that is lightly dusted with icing sugar to between 3 mm/1/8 inch and 5 mm/¼ inch thick and 7 cm/2¾ inches in diameter. Lift over the cake and use your fingers to ease the icing around the sides, pinching it together where there's a point. Cut off the excess at these points and tuck the icing around the base before trimming off excess with a sharp knife.

Making a paper piping bag

Cut out a 25-cm/10-inch square from baking paper and fold it diagonally in half to make a triangle. Cut the paper in half, to one side of the folded line, to make two triangles. Holding one triangle with the long edge away from you, curl the right point over to meet the central point, forming a cone. Curl the left point over the cone. Adjust the points so there's no hole at the tip. Fold the points over to secure the cone in place.

Piping bags and nozzles

Piping bags can be fitted with nozzles or snipped at the tip. Half-fill the bag with icing and twist the open end together to seal. Snip off the tip and test the thickness of the piping, snipping off more if necessary. (If using a piping nozzle, cut 15 mm/½ inch off the tip of the bag and fit with a nozzle before filling and sealing.) The nozzles used in this book are: a large star nozzle for lavish swirls; a small star nozzle for small stars or shells; and a writer nozzle for lines and dots.

Vanilla sponge cake

Makes: 1 x 18-cm/7-inch round or square cake
Prep: 15 minutes
Cook: 40 minutes

When using this moist, buttery sponge cake mixture, follow the baking directions in your chosen recipe. To bake it as a sponge cake, put it in an 18-cm/7-inch round or square greased and lined cake tin and bake for 40 minutes, or until firm to touch.

- 150 g/5½ oz lightly salted butter, softened
- 150 g/5½ oz caster sugar
- 1 tsp vanilla extract
- 3 eggs, beaten
- 175 g/6 oz self-raising flour
- 2 tbsp milk

1. Put the butter and sugar in a mixing bowl and beat them together with an electric handheld whisk until pale and fluffy. Beat in the vanilla. Add the eggs, a little at a time, beating between each addition. (If they are added too quickly, the mixture will separate and the cake won't be as light.)

2. Sift in the flour, then stir it in gently with a metal spoon. As soon as the ingredients are combined, gently stir in the milk. The mixture should drop easily from the spoon when tapped on the side of the bowl. (For a shortcut 'all in one' method, put all the ingredients in the bowl together and beat until soft and creamy.) Cook as per your recipe or turn the mixture out into a greased and lined 18-cm/7-inch cake tin and bake in an oven preheated to 180°C/350°F/Gas Mark 4 for 40 minutes.

Variations

White chocolate:	Replace half the sugar with 200 g/7 oz melted white chocolate, stirring it into the mixture after the eggs.
Lemon:	Add the finely grated rind of 2 lemons when creaming the butter and sugar and use 2 tablespoons of lemon juice instead of vanilla and milk.
Orange:	Add the finely grated rind of 1 orange when creaming the butter and sugar and use 2 tablespoons of orange juice instead of vanilla and milk.
Almond:	Replace 55 g/2 oz flour with 55 g/2 oz ground almonds and add 1 teaspoon of almond extract instead of the vanilla.

Buttercream

Makes: 1 quantity of buttercream

Put 100 g/3½ oz unsalted butter in a mixing bowl and beat with an electric handheld whisk until softened. Add 150 g/5½ oz icing sugar and beat, using the whisk, until smooth and creamy. Pour in 1 tablespoon of hot water and beat again until very soft and fluffy. For vanilla buttercream beat in 1 teaspoon of vanilla extract with the icing sugar. For lemon buttercream beat in the finely grated rind of 1 lemon with the icing sugar and use 2 tablespoons of lemon juice instead of the water.

Mini Classic Cakes

Carrot cakes

Makes: 20
Prep: 1 hour, plus cooling
Cook: 35 minutes

Carrot cake is such an all-time favourite, it quite simply had to be included here. If you're making these in advance, the little marzipan carrots can be positioned after frosting the cake, but don't add the leafy tops more than a few hours before serving as they are likely to wilt.

- 150 g/5½ oz lightly salted butter, softened, plus extra for greasing
- 150 g/5½ oz light muscovado sugar
- 3 eggs
- 150 g/5½ oz self-raising flour
- ½ tsp baking powder
- ½ tsp ground mixed spice
- 85 g/3 oz ground almonds
- finely grated rind of 1 lemon
- 150 g/5½ oz carrots, grated
- 85 g/3 oz sultanas, roughly chopped

DECORATION

- 150 g/5½ oz cream cheese
- 40 g/1½ oz unsalted butter, softened
- 115 g/4 oz icing sugar, plus extra for dusting
- 2 tbsp lemon juice
- 60 g/2¼ oz marzipan
- orange food colouring
- several sprigs of dill

1. Preheat the oven to 180°C/350°F/Gas Mark 4. Grease and line the base and sides of a 26-cm x 22-cm/10-inch x 8-inch roasting tin or similar sized tin. Grease the baking paper. Put the butter, light muscovado sugar, eggs, flour, baking powder, mixed spice, almonds and lemon rind in a mixing bowl and beat together with an electric handheld whisk until smooth and creamy. Stir in the carrots and sultanas.

2. Turn the mixture out into the tin and level the surface. Bake in the preheated oven for 35 minutes, or until risen and just firm to the touch. Leave in the tin for 10 minutes, then transfer to a wire rack to cool.

3. For the decoration, beat together the cream cheese, butter, icing sugar and lemon juice until creamy. Colour the marzipan deep orange (see page 8). Roll it into a sausage shape on a surface lightly dusted with icing sugar, then divide it into 20 pieces and form each one into a small carrot shape, marking shallow grooves around each with a knife.

4. Using a palette knife, spread the frosting over the cake, taking it almost to the edges. Trim the crusts from the cake to neaten it, then cut it into 20 squares. Place a marzipan carrot on each cake and add a small sprig of dill.

1

4

Cherry and almond loaves

Makes: 12
Prep: 15 minutes, plus cooling
Cook: 20 minutes

A bite-sized mini treat for those who like traditional cakes. If you don't have a silicone loaf tray, use individual metal tins (see page 6) – they're slightly larger and you'll have enough mixture for about 8 cakes, which will need an extra 5 minutes' cooking time.

- 85 g/3 oz lightly salted butter, softened, plus extra for greasing
- 70 g/2½ oz caster sugar
- 1 egg
- 1 egg yolk
- 70 g/2½ oz self-raising flour
- ½ tsp almond extract
- 55 g/2 oz ground almonds
- 55 g/2 oz natural glacé cherries, roughly chopped
- 2 tbsp flaked almonds
- 55 g/2 oz icing sugar
- 2 tsp lemon juice

1. Preheat the oven to 180°C/350°F/Gas Mark 4. Place a 12-section silicone mini loaf tray on a baking tray, or grease and base-line individual mini loaf tins. Put the butter, caster sugar, egg, egg yolk, flour, almond extract and ground almonds in a mixing bowl and beat together with an electric hand-held whisk until smooth and creamy. Stir in the cherries.

2. Using a teaspoon, spoon the mixture into the tray sections and level with the back of the spoon. Break up the flaked almonds slightly by squeezing them in your hands and scatter them over the cake mixture. Bake in the preheated oven for 20 minutes (25 minutes if using tins), or until risen and just firm to the touch. Leave in the tray for 5 minutes, then transfer to a wire rack to cool.

3. Beat the icing sugar and lemon juice together in a small bowl and drizzle over the cakes with a teaspoon. Leave to set.

Mango cakes

Makes: 12
Prep: 15 minutes, plus cooling, plus 2–3 hours soaking
Cook: 20 minutes

70 g/2½ oz dried mango, finely chopped

finely grated rind of 1 orange, plus 3 tbsp juice

25 g/1 oz creamed coconut

85 g/3 oz lightly salted butter, softened, plus extra for greasing

70 g/2½ oz caster sugar

1 egg

85 g/3 oz self-raising flour

icing sugar for dusting

Dried mango and creamed coconut give these little tea cakes a fresh, tropical flavour, heightened by a subtle hint of orange. Moist and buttery, they'll keep in an airtight container for several days.

1. Preheat the oven to 180°C/350°F/Gas Mark 4. Place a 12-section silicone mini loaf tray on a baking tray, or grease and base-line individual mini loaf tins. Put the mango and orange juice in a small bowl and leave to stand, covered, for 2–3 hours, or until the orange juice is mostly absorbed. Finely grate the coconut (if it's very firm and difficult to grate, warm it briefly in the microwave first).

2. Put the coconut, butter, sugar, egg, flour and orange rind in a mixing bowl and beat together with an electric handheld whisk until smooth and pale. Stir in the mango and any unabsorbed orange juice.

3. Using a teaspoon, spoon the mixture into the tray sections and level with the back of the spoon. Bake in the preheated oven for 20 minutes (25 minutes if using tins), or until risen and just firm to the touch. Leave in the tray for 5 minutes, then transfer to a wire rack to cool.

4. Serve lightly dusted with icing sugar.

Mini Victoria sandwich cakes

Makes: 12
Prep: 20 minutes, plus cooling
Cook: 15 minutes

So tiny and dainty, these 'doll's house'-sized sponges are just right with a cup of tea when you don't want anything too rich or filling. Because of their size they'll dry out quickly, so store them in an airtight container or freeze if making ahead.

- 70 g/2½ oz lightly salted butter, softened, plus extra for greasing
- 70 g/2½ oz caster sugar
- 70 g/2½ oz self-raising flour
- 1 egg
- 1 egg yolk
- 1 tsp vanilla extract

DECORATION

- 150 ml/5 fl oz double cream
- 6 tbsp strawberry jam
- 85 g/3 oz icing sugar
- 1 tbsp lemon juice

1. Preheat the oven to 180°C/350°F/Gas Mark 4. Place a 12-section silicone mini muffin tray on a baking tray, or grease and base-line a 12-section mini muffin tin. Put the butter, caster sugar, flour, egg, egg yolk and vanilla in a mixing bowl and beat together with an electric handheld whisk until it is smooth and creamy.

2. Using a teaspoon, spoon the mixture into the tray sections and level with the back of the spoon. Bake in the preheated oven for 15 minutes, or until risen and just firm to the touch. Leave in the tray for 5 minutes, then transfer to a wire rack to cool.

3. For the decoration, whip the cream until it just peaks. Split the cakes in half horizontally using a small serrated knife. Press 2 tablespoons of the jam through a small sieve into a bowl to extract the seeds. Put the sieved jam in a small paper piping bag and snip off the tip (see page 8). Sandwich the cakes together with the remaining jam and cream.

4. Beat the icing sugar and lemon juice together in a bowl until smooth. Spoon the icing over the cakes, spreading it just to the edges. Pipe dots of jam on top of each cake and draw a wooden skewer through them.

Iced baby bundt cakes

Makes: 12
Prep: 20 minutes, plus cooling
Cook: 15–20 minutes

This bundt recipe is made with cinnamon, walnuts and apples for a really moist texture. Don't be put off if you don't have mini bundt tins; any small tins with a similar capacity can be used just as effectively.

- 200 g/7 oz plain flour, plus extra for sprinkling
- 1 tsp baking powder
- 1 tsp ground cinnamon, plus extra for sprinkling
- 125 g/4½ oz caster sugar
- 60 g/2¼ oz walnuts, finely chopped
- 2 small dessert apples, peeled, cored and finely grated
- 6 tbsp vegetable oil, plus extra for greasing
- 3 eggs
- 150 ml/5 fl oz buttermilk

ICING

- 3 tbsp natural yogurt
- 150 g/5½ oz icing sugar, sifted

1. Preheat the oven to 180°C/350°F/Gas Mark 4. Brush 2 x 75-ml/2½-fl oz mini bundt tins with vegetable oil. Sprinkle a little flour into the tins and tilt so that both the bases and sides are coated; tap out the excess.

2. Sift the flour, baking powder and cinnamon into a mixing bowl. Stir in the caster sugar, walnuts and apples.

3. In a separate mixing bowl, beat together the oil, eggs and buttermilk. Add them to the dry ingredients and mix to form a soft paste.

4. Using a teaspoon, spoon the mixture into the tins and level with the back of the spoon. Bake in the preheated oven for 15–20 minutes, or until risen and just firm to the touch. Leave in the tins for 5 minutes, then transfer to a wire rack to cool.

5. For the icing, put the yogurt into a bowl and add the icing sugar. Beat together well until smooth. Spoon a little of the icing onto the top of each cake, easing it slightly down the sides with the back of the spoon so the icing runs down the flutes around the sides. Lightly sprinkle the tops of the cakes with cinnamon.

1

2

Coffee crumb cakes

Makes: 18
Prep: 30 minutes, plus cooling
Cook: 30–35 minutes

55 g/2 oz lightly salted butter, softened, plus extra for greasing

100 g/3½ oz caster sugar

1 egg

5 tbsp soured cream

125 g/4½ oz self-raising flour

TOPPING

85 g/3 oz plain flour

70 g/2½ oz lightly salted butter, cut into pieces

½ tsp ground mixed spice

1½ tsp ground espresso coffee

70 g/2½ oz caster sugar

ICING

85 g/3 oz icing sugar

1 tbsp strong espresso coffee

One of these treats is an ideal accompaniment to a mid-morning cup of tea or coffee. The crumb topping is sweet and streusel-like, in delicious contrast to the light and airy sponge underneath it.

1. Preheat the oven to 180°C/350°F/Gas Mark 4. Grease and line the base and sides of an 18-cm/7-inch shallow, loose-bottomed square cake tin. Grease the baking paper.

2. For the topping, put the plain flour, butter, mixed spice and coffee in a food processor and blend until the mixture starts to resemble coarse breadcrumbs. Add the caster sugar and blend again briefly. Tip the mixture into a mixing bowl.

3. For the sponge, put the butter, caster sugar, egg, soured cream and self-raising flour in the food processor and blend until smooth and creamy, then turn out into the tin and level the surface. Sprinkle the crumb mixture in an even layer on top. Bake in the preheated oven for 30–35 minutes, or until risen and just firm to the touch and a skewer inserted into the centre comes out clean. Leave in the tin for 10 minutes, then transfer to a wire rack to cool.

4. For the icing, put all but 2 tablespoons of the icing sugar in a small mixing bowl and add the coffee. Beat to a smooth paste that falls in a thick trail from the spoon, adding a little more icing sugar if necessary. Cut the cake into 3 even-sized pieces, then cut across to make 18 rectangular pieces. Drizzle with the icing.

3

4

Gooey chocolate fudge bites

Makes: 21
Prep: 25 minutes, plus cooling
Cook: 35 minutes

This is as rich and delicious as chocolate cake can be! It's moist and gooey, with a generous amount of chocolate fudge icing. Store in a cool place rather than in the fridge so that the texture doesn't spoil.

- 200 g/7 oz lightly salted butter, cut into pieces, plus extra for greasing
- 200 g/7 oz plain chocolate, roughly chopped
- 100 ml/3½ fl oz double cream
- 3 eggs
- 150 g/5½ oz light muscovado sugar
- 100 g/3½ oz self-raising flour

ICING

- 200 g/7 oz plain chocolate
- 3 tbsp golden syrup
- 55 g/2 oz unsalted butter, cut into pieces
- 70 g/2½ oz icing sugar, sifted

1. Preheat the oven to 160°C/325°F/Gas Mark 3. Grease and line the base and sides of a 20-cm/8-inch square cake tin. Grease the baking paper.

2. Put the butter, chocolate and cream in a heatproof bowl, set the bowl over a saucepan of gently simmering water and heat until melted. Leave to cool slightly.

3. Put the eggs and light muscovado sugar in a mixing bowl and beat together with an electric handheld whisk until the mixture begins to turn frothy. Stir in the cooled chocolate mixture. Sift in the flour and stir it in gently.

4. Turn the mixure into the tin and level the surface. Bake in the preheated oven for 35 minutes, or until risen and just firm to the touch. Leave in the tin for 10 minutes, then transfer to a wire rack to cool.

5. For the icing, put 175 g/6 oz of the chocolate in a small heavy-bottomed saucepan with the syrup and butter. Heat gently, stirring frequently, until the mixture is smooth and glossy. Transfer the mixture to a mixing bowl and beat in the icing sugar. Leave until the icing has thickened enough to just hold its shape.

6. Split the cake in half horizontally and spread half the fudge icing on the cut side of the bottom piece. Place the other piece on top, cut-side down, and spread the remaining icing on top of the cake. Using a sharp knife, carefully cut thin shards from the remaining chocolate. (If it's too brittle, heat very briefly in the microwave and try again.) Trim off the edges of the cake to neaten it, then cut it into 21 rectangles. Scatter the shards on top.

Chocolate brownies

Makes: 25
Prep: 15 minutes, plus cooling
Cook: 18–20 minutes

These little brownies have the familiar sugary crust and soft gooey centre that we've come to know and love. They're impossible to resist, so it's a good thing they're only bite-sized!

- 115 g/4 oz lightly salted butter, cut into pieces, plus extra for greasing
- 100 g/3½ oz plain chocolate, roughly chopped
- 2 eggs
- 175 g/6 oz light muscovado sugar
- 2 tsp vanilla extract
- 55 g/2 oz plain flour
- 25 g/1 oz cocoa powder
- 40 g/1½ oz pecan or walnuts, roughly chopped

1. Preheat the oven to 200°C/400°F/Gas Mark 6. Grease and line the base and sides of an 18-cm/7-inch shallow, loose-bottomed square cake tin.

2. Put the butter and chocolate in a heatproof bowl, set the bowl over a saucepan of gently simmering water and heat until melted. Leave the mixture to cool slightly.

3. Put the eggs, sugar and vanilla in a mixing bowl and beat together with an electric handheld whisk until the mixture begins to turn frothy. Stir in the chocolate mixture until combined.

4. Sift the flour and cocoa powder into the bowl and scatter in the nuts. Stir together gently, then turn the mixture into the tin and level the surface.

5. Bake in the preheated oven for 18–20 minutes, or until the crust feels dry but gives a little when gently pressed. (If you're unsure, it's better to slightly under-cook brownies as they lose their gooeyness when they are over-baked.) Leave in the tin for 10 minutes, then transfer to a wire rack to cool. Cut the cake into 25 squares.

3

4

5

Vanilla swirled brownies

Makes: 12
Prep: 20 minutes, plus cooling
Cook: 12–15 minutes

- 85 g/3 oz lightly salted butter, plus extra for greasing
- 100 g/3½ oz plain chocolate, roughly chopped
- 1 egg
- 1 egg yolk
- 100 g/3½ oz light muscovado sugar
- 40 g/1½ oz self-raising flour
- ¼ tsp baking powder
- 85 g/3 oz milk chocolate, roughly chopped

FROSTING

- 150 g/5½ oz mascarpone cheese
- 4 tbsp icing sugar
- 1 tsp vanilla extract
- milk or plain chocolate curls, to sprinkle

These rich, chocolatey morsels are great as a teatime treat – and even better with coffee after a special dinner with friends.

1. Preheat the oven to 190°C/375°F/Gas Mark 5. Grease and base-line a 12-section mini muffin tin.

2. Put the butter and plain chocolate in a heatproof bowl, set the bowl over a saucepan of gently simmering water and heat until melted. Leave the mixture to cool slightly.

3. Put the egg, egg yolk and light muscovado sugar in a mixing bowl and beat together with an electric handheld whisk until the mixture begins to turn frothy. Stir in the melted chocolate. Sift the flour and baking powder into the bowl, scatter in the milk chocolate and stir together. Using a teaspoon, spoon the mixture into the tray sections.

4. Bake in the preheated oven for 12–15 minutes, or until the crust feels dry but gives a little when gently pressed. (If you're unsure, it's better to slightly under-cook brownies as they lose their gooeyness when over-baked.) Leave in the tray for 10 minutes, then transfer to a wire rack to cool.

5. For the frosting, put the mascarpone cheese, icing sugar and vanilla in a small bowl and beat with an electric handheld whisk until smooth and creamy. Put the mixture in a piping bag fitted with a 1-cm/½-inch star nozzle and pipe swirls over the cakes. Sprinkle with chocolate curls.

Tiny Muffins and Cupcakes

Blueberry and vanilla muffins

Makes: 18
Prep: 10 minutes, plus cooling
Cook: 15 minutes

In these fresh blueberry muffins, the plump, juicy fruits burst during baking to colour and flavour the light, airy sponge. This recipe uses homemade paper cases, made by pressing squares of baking paper into the muffin tray.

- 125 g/4½ oz self-raising flour
- ½ tsp baking powder
- 70 g/2½ oz caster sugar
- 85 g/3 oz blueberries
- 2 tsp vanilla extract
- 1 egg
- 125 ml/4 fl oz buttermilk
- 2 tbsp vegetable oil
- vanilla sugar, for dusting

1. Preheat the oven to 190°C/375°F/Gas Mark 5. Cut out 18 x 9-cm/3½-inch squares from baking paper. Push the squares into 2 x 12-section mini muffin tins, creasing the squares to fit so that they form paper cases. Don't worry if they lift out of the sections slightly; the weight of the muffin mixture will hold them in place.

2. Sift the flour and baking powder into a mixing bowl. Stir in the sugar and blueberries. In a separate mixing bowl, beat together the vanilla, egg, buttermilk and oil with a fork until evenly combined.

3. Tip the buttermilk mixture into the flour. Using a dessertspoon, gently fold the ingredients together until only just mixed. (Don't over-blend the ingredients or the muffins won't be as light.)

4. Spoon the mixture into the paper cases; it should be level with the top of the tin. Sprinkle with a little vanilla sugar and bake in the preheated oven for 15 minutes, or until risen and just firm to the touch. Leave the muffins in the tin for 2 minutes, then transfer them in their cases to a wire rack to cool. Serve warm or cold, dusted with extra vanilla sugar.

Cranberry muffins

Makes: 18
Prep: 10 minutes, plus cooling
Cook: 12–15 minutes

These muffins can be prepared and baked in less than half an hour, perfect for a relaxed weekend breakfast. For flavour variations, try adding the grated rind of an orange or a sprinkling of ground ginger or cinnamon.

- 100 g/3½ oz self-raising flour
- ½ tsp baking powder
- 55 g/2 oz caster sugar
- 100 g/3½ oz dried cranberries, roughly chopped
- 100 ml/3½ fl oz natural yogurt
- 1 egg
- 2 tbsp vegetable oil
- icing sugar, for dusting

1. Preheat the oven to 190°C/375°F/Gas Mark 5. Line 2 x 12-section mini muffin tins with 18 x 3-cm/1¼-inch mini paper cases.

2. Sift the flour and baking powder into a mixing bowl. Stir in the caster sugar and cranberries. In a separate mixing bowl, beat together the yogurt, egg and vegetable oil with a fork until evenly combined.

3. Tip the yogurt mixture into the flour. Using a dessertspoon, gently fold the ingredients together until only just mixed. (Don't over-blend the ingredients or the muffins won't be as light.)

4. Spoon the mixture into the paper cases; it should be level with the top of the tin. Bake in the preheated oven for 12–15 minutes, or until risen and just firm to the touch. Leave the muffins in the tin for 2 minutes, then transfer them in their cases to a wire rack to cool. Serve warm or cold, dusted with icing sugar.

2

3

4

Double chocolate muffins

Makes: 12
Prep: 15 minutes, plus cooling
Cook: 15 minutes

Because these muffins are tiny, it's only right that they're as packed with chocolate as they could be! Any that are not eaten fresh from the oven can be kept for two days in an airtight container. Warm them for a few minutes in a moderate oven to revive their flavour.

- 15 g/½ oz cocoa powder
- 70 g/2½ oz self-raising flour
- ¼ tsp baking powder
- 25 g/1 oz light muscovado sugar
- 85 g/3 oz milk chocolate, roughly chopped
- 1 egg
- 3 tbsp milk
- 40 g/1½ oz lightly salted butter, melted
- 40 g/1½ oz plain chocolate, roughly chopped

1. Preheat the oven to 190°C/375°F/Gas Mark 5. Line a 12-section mini muffin tin with 3-cm/1¼-inch mini paper cases.

2. Sift the cocoa powder, flour and baking powder into a mixing bowl. Stir in the light muscovado sugar and milk chocolate. In a separate mixing bowl, beat together the egg, milk and butter with a fork until they are evenly combined.

3. Tip the egg mixture into the flour. Using a dessertspoon, gently fold the ingredients together until only just mixed. (Don't over-blend the ingredients or the muffins won't be as light.)

4. Spoon the mixture into the paper cases; it should be level with the top of the tin. Bake in the preheated oven for 15 minutes, or until risen and just firm to the touch. Leave the muffins in the tin for 2 minutes, then transfer them in their cases to a wire rack to cool.

5. Put the plain chocolate in a heatproof bowl, set over a saucepan of gently simmering water and heat until melted. Using a teaspoon, drizzle the melted chocolate over the muffins and serve warm or cold.

4

5

Maple and banana cupcakes

Makes: 12
Prep: 20 minutes, plus cooling
Cook: 18–20 minutes

Banana cake invariably appeals to everyone, from tiny tots to adults. These mini ones can be served plain, simply dusted with icing sugar, or swirled with the delicious maple butter frosting.

- 1 small banana
- 2 tbsp maple syrup
- 2 tbsp milk
- 60 g/2¼ oz lightly salted butter, softened
- 70 g/2½ oz caster sugar
- 1 egg, beaten
- 100 g/3½ oz self-raising flour

FROSTING

- 150 g/5½ oz lightly salted butter, softened
- 1 tsp vanilla extract
- 6 tbsp icing sugar
- 7 tbsp maple syrup
- 8 pecan or walnut halves, roughly chopped, to decorate

1. Preheat the oven to 180°C/350°F/Gas Mark 4. Line a 12-section mini muffin tin with 3-cm/1¼-inch mini paper cases.

2. In a small mixing bowl, mash the banana to a purée with a fork. Stir in the maple syrup and milk.

3. Put the butter and caster sugar in a separate mixing bowl and beat together with an electric handheld whisk until light and fluffy. Gradually beat in the egg, a little at a time, adding a teaspoon of the flour if the mixture starts to separate.

4. Sift half the flour into the bowl containing the butter mixture, then add half the banana. Gently fold the ingredients together until only just mixed. Sift in the remaining flour, add the remaining banana mixture and fold in.

5. Spoon the mixture into the paper cases. Bake in the preheated oven for 18–20 minutes, or until risen and just firm to the touch. Leave in the tin for 5 minutes, then transfer to a wire rack to cool.

6. For the frosting, put the butter, vanilla, icing sugar and maple syrup in a bowl and beat with an electric handheld whisk until smooth and creamy. Put the frosting in a small paper piping bag fitted with a 1-cm/½-inch star nozzle and use to decorate the cupcakes. Scatter with the nuts.

2

4

Almond daisy cupcakes

Makes: 12
Prep: 25 minutes, plus cooling
Cook: 12–15 minutes

- 3 egg whites
- 40 g/1½ oz plain flour
- 85 g/3 oz icing sugar
- 70 g/2½ oz ground almonds
- 70 g/2½ oz lightly salted butter, melted and cooled

DECORATION

- 1 quantity Lemon Buttercream (see page 9)
- red, black and lime green food colourings
- 55 g/2 oz whole blanched almonds
- 6 red and 6 black mini jelly beans

These fun flower cupcakes will add a welcome splash of springtime colour to the tea table. The buttercream topping is fresh and lemony, while the almond cake is moist, nutty and light.

1. Preheat the oven to 200°C/400°F/Gas Mark 6. Line a 12-section mini muffin tin with 3-cm/1¼-inch mini paper cases, preferably in red or black.

2. Whisk the eggs whites in a clean mixing bowl until they're broken up but not fluffy. Add the flour, sugar, ground almonds and butter and stir together to make a smooth paste. Spoon the mixture into the paper cases. Bake in the preheated oven for 12–15 minutes, or until risen and just firm to the touch. Leave in the tin for 5 minutes, then transfer to a wire rack.

3. For the decoration, spoon 2 tablespoons of the buttercream into a small bowl and colour with red food colouring. Spoon a further 2 tablespoons into another bowl and colour black. Colour the remaining buttercream lime green, and spread this over the cakes with a palette knife.

4. Using a sharp knife, carefully cut each blanched almond in half to make flat petal shapes. Press a jelly bean into the centre of each cake and surround with almonds, pressing them gently into the buttercream in order to shape flowers.

5. Put the red buttercream in a small paper piping bag and the black in another, and snip off the tips (see page 8). Pipe an outline around the edges of each almond, half in red and half in black.

Baby shower cupcakes

Makes: 18
Prep: 45 minutes, plus cooling
Cook: 15 minutes

70 g/2½ oz lightly salted butter, softened

70 g/2½ oz caster sugar

1 egg

1 egg yolk

70 g/2½ oz self-raising flour

1 tsp vanilla extract

DECORATION

1 quantity Buttercream (see page 90)

pink and blue food colourings

55 g/2 oz ready-to-roll icing

icing sugar, for dusting

These are so simple to make, but very pretty – and perfect for the next baby shower. Pink and blue look effective together, but you can change the colour scheme to any other combination.

1. Preheat the oven to 180°C/350°F/Gas Mark 4. Line 2 x 12-section mini muffin tins with 18 x 3-cm/1¼-inch mini paper cases, preferably in deep pink or blue.

2. Put the butter, caster sugar, egg, egg yolk, flour and vanilla in a mixing bowl and beat together with an electric handheld whisk until smooth and creamy. Spoon the mixture into the paper cases. Bake in the preheated oven for 15 minutes, or until risen and just firm to the touch. Leave in the tin for 5 minutes, then transfer to a wire rack to cool.

3. For the decoration, divide the buttercream equally between 2 bowls and colour 1 with pink colouring and the other with blue, so they're pale pastel. Using a palette knife, spread a thin layer of pink icing over half the cakes and blue over the other half, reserving some for decoration.

4. Colour the remaining buttercream in the bowls to a deeper tone and put it in small paper piping bags fitted with 1-cm/½-inch star nozzles. Pipe pink shells around the blue cakes and blue shells around the pink ones.

5. Colour half the ready-to-roll icing blue (see page 8) and wrap it tightly in clingfilm. Colour the remainder pink and roll it out thinly on a surface lightly dusted with icing sugar.

6. Cut the pink icing into 1-cm/½-inch wide strips, then cut across these at 2.5-cm/1-inch intervals to make tiny rectangles. Use 2 rectangles to shape bow ends, pinching the ends together as you position them on the blue-edged cakes. Bend 2 more rectangles into loops, pinching the ends together, and secure with a damp paintbrush to complete each bow. Use the blue icing in the same way to make bows for the pink-edged cakes.

Chocolate and raspberry cupcakes

Makes: 20
Prep: 50 minutes, plus cooling
Cook: 12–15 minutes

- 70 g/2½ oz raspberries
- 55 g/2 oz cocoa powder
- 100 ml/3½ fl oz boiling water
- 55 g/2 oz lightly salted butter, softened
- 125 g/4½ oz light muscovado sugar
- 1 egg, beaten
- 100 g/3½ oz self-raising flour

DECORATION

- 40 g/1½ oz lightly salted butter
- 100 g/3½ oz plain chocolate, roughly chopped
- 2 tbsp golden syrup
- 40 g/1½ oz raspberries
- 85 g/3 oz icing sugar, sifted

Here's your chance to get carried away with special messages on these pretty cakes – hearts, kisses, whatever you fancy! Once decorated they'll keep fresh for a couple of days in a cool place.

1. Preheat the oven to 180°C/350°F/Gas Mark 4. Line 2 x 12-section mini muffin tins with 20 x 3-cm/1¼-inch mini paper cases, preferably in deep pink or brown.

2. Put the raspberries in a small mixing bowl and crush with a fork until they are broken up. In a separate mixing bowl, whisk the cocoa powder with the boiling water. Leave to cool.

3. Put the butter and light muscovado sugar in a third mixing bowl and beat together with an electric handheld whisk until light and fluffy. Beat in the egg a little at a time.

4. Stir in the flour and the cocoa mixture until evenly combined, then add the raspberries and mix together lightly. Spoon the mixture into the paper cases. Bake in the preheated oven for 12–15 minutes, or until risen and just firm to the touch. Leave in the tins for 5 minutes, then transfer to a wire rack to cool.

5. For the decoration, melt the butter in a small saucepan and add the chocolate and syrup. Heat very gently until the chocolate has almost melted, then tip into a mixing bowl. Leave to cool, stirring frequently, until the mixture has thickened enough to almost hold its shape. Spoon it over the cakes and spread to the edges using a palette knife.

6. Crush the raspberries and press them through a sieve, using the back of a spoon to extract the juice. Sift the icing sugar over the juice and stir to make a loose paste. Put the icing in a small paper piping bag and snip off the tip (see page 8). Pipe hearts and kisses onto the cakes.

Red velvet heart cupcakes

Makes: 12
Prep: 1–1½ hours, plus cooling
Cook: 15 minutes

1 small raw beetroot, about 70 g/2½ oz, finely grated

1 egg

2 tbsp buttermilk or soured cream

1 tsp vinegar

55 g/2 oz lightly salted butter, softened

25 g/1 oz light muscovado sugar

55 g/2 oz self-raising flour

2 tsp cocoa powder

DECORATION

½ quantity Buttercream (see page 9)

70 g/2½ oz ready-to-roll icing

deep red food colouring

icing sugar for dusting

These cakes take a little while to decorate, but the results are gorgeous. Make yourself comfortable and enjoy!

1. Preheat the oven to 180°C/350°F/Gas Mark 4. Line a 12-section mini muffin tin with 4-cm/1½-inch mini paper cases, in deep red or white.

2. Put the beetroot, egg, buttermilk and vinegar in a mixing bowl and stir together until well combined. Put the butter and light muscovado sugar in a separate mixing bowl and beat together with an electric handheld whisk until pale and fluffy. Sift half the flour and cocoa powder into the butter mixture and tip in the beetroot mixture. Stir gently until evenly combined. Sift in the remaining flour and cocoa and stir again to mix.

3. Spoon the mixture into the paper cases. Bake in the preheated oven for 15 minutes, or until risen and just firm to the touch. Leave in the tin for 5 minutes, then transfer to a wire rack to cool.

4. For the decoration, spread the buttercream over the cakes using a palette knife. Colour the ready-to-roll icing deep red (see page 8).

5. Roll a 5 g/⅛ oz piece of icing into a thin rope 12 cm/4½ inches long. On a surface lightly dusted with icing sugar, flatten it with a rolling pin, keeping it no more than 1-cm/½-inch wide. Cut it in half lengthways, then across into 2.5-cm/1-inch pieces. Roll each little piece up between your thumb and finger to resemble a tiny rose. Use the roses to build heart shapes on top of all the cakes by pressing them gently down into the buttercream.

Petite Party Cakes

Summer flower cakes

Makes: 16
Prep: 2½ hours, plus cooling
Cook: 25 minutes

These little cakes are a labour of love, but look simply stunning. If you've planned a colour scheme for a special party, you can alter the colours of the vertical stripes to enhance your theme. Once decorated, they'll keep in a cool place for several days.

- a little lightly salted butter, for greasing
- 1 quantity Lemon Sponge mixture (see page 9)
- 1 quantity Lemon Buttercream (see page 9)
- 900 g/2 lb white ready-to-roll icing
- pink and purple food colourings
- icing sugar, for dusting

1. Preheat the oven to 180°C/350°F/Gas Mark 4. Grease and base-line a cake tin containing 16 x 5-cm/2-inch sections.

2. Put a dessertspoon of the sponge mixture into each tin section. (If you have digital scales, make sure you put exactly the same amount in each section. To do this, put the prepared tin on the scales and set them to zero, then spoon 35 g/1¼ oz mixture into a section, reset the scales to zero, and fill the remaining sections, resetting the scales each time.) Bake in the preheated oven for 25 minutes, or until risen and just firm to the touch. Leave in the tin for 5 minutes before carefully loosening each cake by running a slender knife around the sides of each section. Transfer the cakes to a wire rack to cool before peeling away the base paper.

3. Reserve 3 tablespoons of the buttercream and use the remainder to spread a thin layer over the tops and sides of the cakes.

4. Reserve 300 g/10½ oz of the ready-to-roll icing. From the remainder, colour 200 g/7 oz pale pink, 200 g/7 oz purple and 200 g/7 oz a darker pink (see page 8). Take half of each coloured icing and roll it out thinly on a surface lightly dusted with icing sugar. Cut a strip from each colour that is the depth of the cakes. Cut this into 5-mm/¼-inch wide strips the depth of the cake and secure them, in alternating colours, around the sides of the cakes, pressing them gently into the buttercream. Use the remaining coloured icings to cover all the cakes.

5. Roll out the reserved white ready-to-roll icing as thinly as possible on a surface lightly dusted with icing sugar and cut out simple flower shapes using a 15-mm/½-inch plunger cutter. Press each cut flower shape out onto your finger and then place it on top of a cake. Repeat until you've built up a cluster of flowers on one cake, then repeat for all the cakes.

6. Colour the reserved buttercream pink. Put it in a small paper piping bag and snip off the tip (see page 8). Pipe little dots in the centres of all the white flowers.

White party stars

Makes: 9–10
Prep: 1–1 ½ hours, plus cooling
Cook: 25–30 minutes

unsalted butter, for greasing

1 quantity Orange Sponge mixture (see page 9)

1 quantity Orange Buttercream (see page 9)

400 g/14 oz white ready-to-roll icing

1 egg white

200 g/7 oz icing sugar, sifted, plus extra for dusting

lilac food colouring

These pretty little stars would make a great addition to a special occasion; you could substitute the colour of your choice to tie in with your party theme.

1. Preheat the oven to 180°C/350°F/Gas Mark 4. Grease and line the base and sides of a 26-cm x 22-cm/10½-inch x 8½-inch roasting tin or similar sized tin.

2. Turn the sponge mixture into the tin and level the surface. Bake in the preheated oven for 25–30 minutes, or until risen and just firm to the touch. Leave in the tin for 10 minutes, then transfer to a wire rack to cool.

3. If the cake has risen in the centre, cut off a thin slice with a large knife. Using an 8-cm/3-inch star cutter as a guide, cut out shapes from the sponge. (Cut each star shape as close to the previously cut star as possible so you don't waste any sponge; freeze the sponge trimmings for making trifle or cake pops another time.) Turn the cakes over so that the base forms a flat top.

4. Using a palette knife, spread a thin layer of buttercream over the top and sides of each star.

5. Roll out 40 g/1½ oz ready-to-roll icing on a surface lightly dusted with icing sugar to a circle roughly 11 cm/4½ inches in diameter. Lift it over a star cake and fit the sides, pinching the icing together at the points. Cut off the excess at the points and then cut around the base of the cake. Repeat with the remaining cakes.

6. Beat the egg white in a clean bowl with the half the icing sugar until smooth. Gradually work in the remaining icing sugar until softly peaking. Add a little lilac food colouring and put the icing in a small paper piping bag fitted with a little writer nozzle (see page 8). Pipe tiny dots in the centre of the tops of the cakes.

Birthday balloons

Makes: 24
Prep: 1–1½ hours, plus cooling
Cook: 18–20 minutes

1 quantity White Chocolate Sponge mixture (see page 9)

2 quantities Buttercream (see page 9)

350 g/12 oz chewy sweets in 3 flavours, e.g. blackcurrant, strawberry and orange

24 x 6-cm/2½-inch lolly sticks

100 g/3½ oz small red, green and yellow candy-coated chocolate sweets, such as M&Ms

Kids will love these fun, colourful cakes, lavishly decorated with tempting treats. Use candles to replace some of the balloons if you prefer.

1. Preheat the oven to 180°C/350°F/Gas Mark 4. Line 2 x 12-section mini muffin tins with 4-cm/1½-inch mini paper cases, preferably in pink, green or yellow.

2. Spoon the cake mixture into the paper cases. Bake in the preheated oven for 18–20 minutes, until risen and just firm to the touch. Leave in the tin for 5 minutes, then transfer to a wire rack to cool.

3. Using a palette knife, spread a thin layer of buttercream over the cakes.

4. For each balloon, take 8 g/⅙ oz chewy sweets (about 2 sweets) and mould them into a ball. (If they are brittle or too firm to shape, microwave them on medium power for 5–6 seconds to soften them first. Don't overheat them or they'll turn to a molten syrup.) Push each balloon shape onto the end of a lolly stick. Pinch the sweet around the stick to create the effect of a knotted end. Repeat until you have enough balloons, pushing each into a cake.

5. For the streamers, soften the remaining chewy sweets as above and roll them out thinly. Cut them into 5-cm/2-inch x 5-mm/¼-inch pieces and curl each one around a lolly stick. Twist the sweets off the sticks. Scatter the cakes with the candy-coated sweets and the sweet twists to finish.

4

5

Mini party cakes

Makes: 16
Prep: 1¼ hours, plus cooling
Cook: 40 minutes

A platter of these delicious cakes will look impressive at any special get-together. Make them a couple of days in advance, so you've got time to enjoy the decorating before more pressing party tasks arise. For a big birthday use number sparklers too.

- a little lightly salted butter, for greasing
- 1 quantity Vanilla Sponge mixture (see page 9)
- 1 quantity Vanilla Buttercream (see page 9)
- heart-shaped sugar sprinkles
- pearl balls

1. Preheat the oven to 180°C/350°F/Gas Mark 4. Grease and line the base and sides of an 18-cm/7-inch square cake tin.

2. Spoon the cake mixture into the tin and level the surface with the back of the spoon. Bake in the preheated oven for 40 minutes, or until risen and just firm to the touch. Leave in the tin for 10 minutes, then transfer to a wire rack to cool.

3. Cut a 1-cm/½-inch crust off the edges of the cake, then cut the cake into 16 even-sized squares.

4. Put the buttercream in a paper piping bag fitted with a small star nozzle (see page 8). Place the cakes in paper cake cases.

5. Pipe vertical lines down the sides and over the top edges of the cakes. Scatter the tops of the cakes with sugar sprinkles and pearl balls.

3

5

Pupcakes

Makes: 12
Prep: 1½ hours, plus cooling
Cook: 15 minutes

Chewy sweets are brilliant for shaping and modelling cake decorations. These cute little puppy faces will provide plenty of fun at a kids' party or special tea – the kids can even help you make them!

- 70 g/2½ oz lightly salted butter, softened, plus extra for greasing
- 55 g/2 oz caster sugar
- 70 g/2½ oz self-raising flour
- 1 egg
- 1 egg yolk
- 1 tsp vanilla extract
- 25 g/1 oz white chocolate, finely chopped

DECORATION

- 300 g/10½ oz fondant icing sugar
- 3 tbsp cold water
- blue and black food colourings
- 16 white chewy sweets
- 8 black chewy sweets
- ½ quantity Buttercream (see page 9)
- small piece pink chewy sweet
- small piece yellow chewy sweet

1. Preheat the oven to 180°C/350°F/Gas Mark 4. Place a 12-section silicone mini muffin tray on a baking tray, or grease and base-line a 12-section mini muffin tin. Put the butter, caster sugar, flour, egg, egg yolk and vanilla in a mixing bowl and beat together with an electric handheld whisk until smooth and creamy. Stir in the chocolate.

2. Using a teapoon, spoon the mixture into the tray sections and level with the back of the spoon. Bake in the preheated oven for 15 minutes, or until risen and just firm to the touch. Leave in the tray for 5 minutes, then transfer to a wire rack to cool.

3. For the decoration, put the fondant icing sugar in a bowl and beat in 2 tablespoons of the water. Add the third tablespoon gradually, stirring with a wooden spoon until the icing is smooth and slowly drips off the back of the spoon. Stir in a little blue food colouring.

4. Dip a cake into the icing until coated. Lift the cake out of the bowl on a fork and let the excess icing drip back into the bowl before transferring the cake to the wire rack. Repeat with the remaining cakes.

5. Using a rolling pin, flatten the white chewy sweets one at a time. (If they are brittle or too firm to shape, microwave them on medium power for 5–6 seconds to soften them first. Don't overheat them or they'll turn into a molten syrup.) Using scissors, cut out rounds from the white sweets, about 4 cm/1½ inches in diameter, and secure them to the tops of the cakes using a little water.

6. Roll pea-sized balls of black chewy sweets into long, flat 'ears' (softening the sweets first as above if brittle) and position them on the cakes. Use smaller pieces for noses.

7. Beat a little black food colouring into the buttercream. Put it in a paper piping bag and snip off the tip (see page 8). Use to pipe eyes, a mouth and whiskers onto each face. Use the pink chewy sweets to shape tongues and yellow chewy sweets to shape collars. If liked, shape small bones from the leftover white chews and rest them next to the cakes.

Halloween cakes

Makes: 18
Prep: 1½ hours, plus cooling
Cook: 40 minutes

- a little lightly salted butter, for greasing
- 2 quantities Orange Sponge mixture (see page 9)
- 2 tbsp lemon juice
- 2 tbsp orange juice
- 3 tbsp runny honey
- 6 tbsp apricot jam
- 2 tbsp hot water
- orange food colouring
- 750 g/1 lb 10 oz white ready-to-roll icing
- icing sugar, for dusting
- 55 g/2 oz plain chocolate, roughly chopped
- several soft green jellies
- 20 small Oreo cookies, filling removed

Serve these cakes at a Halloween party, or box them up for impressive 'take home' gifts. They look particularly stunning on a dark plate or cloth.

1. Preheat the oven to 180°C/350°F/Gas Mark 4. Grease and line the base and sides of a 26-cm x 22-cm/10½-inch x 8½-inch roasting tin or similar sized tin. Grease the baking paper.

2. Turn the cake mixture into the tin and level the surface. Bake in the preheated oven for 40 minutes, or until risen and just firm to the touch. Leave in the tin for 10 minutes, then transfer to a wire rack to cool.

3. If the cake has risen in the centre, cut off a thin slice with a large knife. Using a 6-cm/2½-inch half-moon cutter as a guide, cut out shapes from the sponge. Turn the cakes over so that the base forms a flat top.

4. Mix the juices with the honey in a small jug and drizzle over the surface of the cakes so the syrup seeps into the sponge. Press the jam through a small sieve into a bowl and stir in the hot water. Brush this mixture over the tops and sides of the cakes.

5. Knead orange food colouring into the ready-to-roll icing (see page 8). Roll out 40 g/1½ oz of the icing on a surface lightly dusted with icing sugar to an oval 15 cm x 10 cm/6 inches x 4 inches. Lift it over a half-moon cake and fit it around the sides, pinching the icing together at the points. Cut off the excess at these points and then cut around the base of the cake. Repeat with the remaining cakes, reserving the icing trimmings.

6. Put the chocolate in a heatproof bowl, set the bowl over a saucepan of gently simmering water and heat until melted. Put the chocolate in a small paper piping bag and snip off the tip (see page 8). Colour the icing trimmings a deeper orange and shape them into small balls. Mark 'pumpkin' ridges with the back of a knife. Cut small pieces of soft jelly and push them into the tops for stalks, securing with chocolate.

7. To shape bats, heat an Oreo cookie in the microwave until it's soft (this will take 1½–2 minutes, but check after a minute). Cut a circle from one side with a 2.5-cm/1-inch cutter. Cut small flutes from the opposite sides with a 1.5-cm/½-inch cutter. Secure the decorations in place with chocolate and pipe bat eyes and extra bats around the sides of the cakes.

Party presents

Makes: 16
Prep: 1½ hours, plus cooling and decorating
Cook: 45 minutes

- a little lightly salted butter, for greasing
- 1 quantity White Chocolate or Almond Sponge mixture (see page 9)
- 1 quantity Buttercream (see page 9)
- 8 tbsp apricot jam
- 2 tbsp brandy, almond or orange liqueur or water
- 850 g/1 lb 14 oz white marzipan
- green, blue and pink food colourings
- icing sugar, for dusting
- 55 g/2 oz white chocolate, roughly chopped
- 3 metres/10 feet deep pink ribbon, about 1-cm/½-inch wide
- 3 metres/10 feet yellow ribbon, about 5-mm/¼-inch wide

Marzipan makes a great cake covering, particularly for those who find the sweetness of icing too much. It can be coloured, rolled, cut out and shaped just as you would ready-to-roll icing, and is equally fun to work with.

1. Preheat the oven to 180°C/350°F/Gas Mark 4. Grease and line the base and sides of an 18-cm/7-inch square cake tin. Turn the cake mixture out into the tin and level the surface. Bake in the preheated oven for 45 minutes, or until risen and just firm to the touch. Leave in the tin for 10 minutes, then transfer to a wire rack to cool.

2. If the cake has risen in the centre, cut off a thin slice with a large knife so that the surface of the cake is level. Split the cake in half horizontally and sandwich the halves together with the buttercream. Cut a 5-mm/¼-inch crust off the sides. Turn the cake over and check that it's completely level. Cut the cake into 16 even-sized squares.

3. Press the jam through a small sieve into a little saucepan and stir in the brandy. Heat gently until smooth. Colour 25 g/1 oz of the marzipan green (see page 8) and another 25 g/1 oz blue and reserve both, wrapped separately in clingfilm. Colour the remaining marzipan pale pink. Brush the apricot glaze all over the tops and sides of the cake squares.

4. Roll out 55 g/2 oz of the pink marzipan thinly on a surface lightly dusted with icing sugar, to a 12-cm/4½-inch square. Lift it over a cake and fit it down the sides, pinching the excess together at the corners. Cut off the excess at these corners and then cut around the base of the cake. Repeat with the remaining cakes, reserving the marzipan trimmings.

5. Colour the marzipan trimmings a deeper shade of pink and use, with the other coloured marzipans, to shape parcels. Arrange on the cakes.

6. Put the chocolate in a heatproof bowl, set the bowl over a saucepan of gently simmering water and heat until melted. Put the melted chocolate in a small paper piping bag and snip off the tip (see page 8). Pipe lines over the parcels and around the top edges of the cakes. Cut the pink ribbon into 19-cm/7½-inch lengths and secure around the bases of the cakes with dots of chocolate from the piping bag. Cut the yellow ribbon into the same sized lengths and position these so they sit in the centre of the pink ribbon, again secured with dots of the chocolate.

Mini ivory wedding cakes

Makes: 16
Prep: 1½ hours, plus cooling
Cook: 1 hour

Make these pretty cakes for a girls' night before the big day, or of course for the wedding party itself. Bake the sponges a day before decorating so they've time to firm up a bit. Assemble the cakes a day before the party.

- a little lightly salted butter, for greasing
- 2 quantities White Chocolate Sponge mixture (see page 9)
- 250 g/9 oz white ready-to-roll icing
- brown or ivory food colouring
- icing sugar, for dusting
- 16 x 7.5-cm/3-inch round silver cake cards
- 300 ml/10 fl oz double cream
- 300 g/10½ oz white chocolate, roughly chopped
- 10 metres (33 feet) wired organza ribbon, about 2.5 cm/1 inch wide

1. Preheat the oven to 180°C/350°F/Gas Mark 4. Grease and line the base and sides of a 23-cm/9-inch square cake tin.

2. Spoon two-thirds of the cake mixture into the tin and level the surface with the back of the spoon. Bake in the preheated oven for 35 minutes, or until well risen and just firm to the touch. Leave in the tin for 10 minutes, then transfer to a wire rack to cool. Wash and reline the tin and bake the remaining mixture for 20–25 minutes, as before.

3. Colour the ready-to-roll icing with a dash of brown food colouring (see page 8). Roll out half the icing as thinly as possible on a surface lightly dusted with icing sugar. Cut out 8 rounds using a 7.5-cm/3-inch cookie cutter, re-rolling the trimmings to make sufficient. Repeat with the other half. Dampen the surfaces of the cake cards and position a circle of icing on each.

4. To make a ganache, heat half the cream in a small saucepan until very hot but not boiling. Pour it into a mixing bowl and add the chocolate. Leave to stand, stirring frequently, until the chocolate has melted. Leave to cool completely. Stir in the remaining cream and beat lightly with an electric handheld whisk on a slow speed until the ganache is just thick enough to hold its shape. (If over-whisked it might start to separate.)

5. Using a 5-cm/2-inch round cookie cutter as a guide, cut out 16 rounds from the deeper sponge cake. Use a 3-cm/1½-inch round cutter as a guide to cut out 16 rounds from the shallower sponge. (Freeze the trimmings for making trifle or cake pops another time.) Place the larger cakes on the iced cards, securing with a little ganache. Spread some of the remaining ganache over the tops and sides of these cakes with a palette knife. Position the smaller cakes on top and cover these with ganache in the same way. Leave to set in a cool place for 1–2 hours.

6. Cut the ribbon into 60-cm/24-inch lengths and wrap a length around each cake, securing at the tops with bows and cutting off any long ends.

Little Fabulous Cakes

Mini cake pops

Makes: 24
Prep: 1–1¼ hours, plus setting
Cook: 40 minutes

These mini 'cupcake' cake pops have both child and adult appeal, so they're ideal for a gathering of mixed ages. Once iced, they'll keep in a cool place for a couple of days.

- 450 g/1 lb cooked Vanilla or Almond Sponge (see page 9) or shop-bought
- 85 g/3 oz mascarpone cheese
- 70 g/2½ oz icing sugar
- ½ tsp vanilla or almond extract

DECORATION

- 225 g/8 oz milk chocolate, roughly chopped
- 24 lolly sticks
- 150 g/5½ oz fondant icing sugar
- pink food colouring
- 4 tsp cold water
- 24 small sweets, such as mini M&Ms
- sugar sprinkles

1. Line a baking tray with baking paper. Crumble the sponge cake into a mixing bowl. Add the mascarpone, icing sugar and vanilla and mix together until you have a thick paste.

2. Roll a 25 g/1 oz piece of the paste into a ball. Push this ball into a mini paper case, pressing it down so that when it is removed from the case you have a mini cupcake shape. Shape the remaining 23 cake pops in the same way. Place on the baking tray and chill for 1–2 hours to firm up.

3. Put the chocolate in a heatproof bowl, set the bowl over a saucepan of gently simmering water and heat until melted. Remove from the heat. Push a lolly stick into each cake pop. Dip a cake pop into the chocolate, turning it until coated. Lift it from the bowl, letting the excess drip back into the bowl, then place it in a cup or tumbler. Repeat with the remaining cake pops. Chill or leave in a cool place until the chocolate has set.

4. Put the fondant icing sugar in a mixing bowl and beat in a dash of pink food colouring and the water until smooth. The icing should almost hold its shape. Spoon a little onto a cake pop, easing it slightly down the sides with the side of a teaspoon. If the icing is too firm you might need to add a dash more water. Before the icing sets, place a small sweet in the centre of each cake pop and scatter with sugar sprinkles.

3

4

Snowman cake pops

Makes: 20

Prep: 1¼–1½ hours, plus setting

200 g/7 oz shop-bought angel cake

300 g/10½ oz icing sugar

4 tbsp double cream

2 tsp peppermint extract

DECORATION

300 g/10½ oz fondant icing sugar, plus extra for piping

20 lolly sticks

3 tbsp cold water

black, orange, red and yellow food colourings

100 g/3½ oz marzipan

Whether it's a winter birthday, Christmas or New Year, these fun seasonal cake pops are perfect – especially if there's snow on the ground!

1. Line a baking tray with baking paper. Crumble the angel cake into a mixing bowl. Add the icing sugar, cream and peppermint extract and mix together until you have a thick paste, adding a dash more cream if the mixture feels too dry.

2. Roll a 20 g/¾ oz piece of the paste into a ball and shape the remaining 19 snowman bases in the same way. Now roll 20 x 5 g/⅛ oz pieces of the paste into balls. Press a small ball onto a larger one to shape a snowman, and repeat for the remaining snowmen. Place on the baking tray and chill for 1–2 hours to firm up.

3. Put the fondant icing sugar in a mixing bowl and beat in the water to make a paste that coats the back of a spoon in a thin layer. Push a lolly stick through each snowman so it goes halfway into the smaller ball (various types of lolly sticks are available; use traditional white or wooden ones; sturdy bamboo skewers can also be used or a pack of chop sticks).

4. Dip a snowman in the icing, turning it until coated. Lift it from the bowl, letting the excess drip back into the bowl, then place it in a cup or tumbler. Repeat with the remaining snowmen, reserving some icing.

5. Beat a dash of black food colouring and a little extra icing sugar into the icing left in the bowl so the mixture is thick enough to hold its shape. Put the icing in a small paper piping bag and snip off the tip (see page 8).

6. Colour a cherry-sized ball of marzipan orange (see page 8), then half the remainder red and half yellow. Use the red and yellow marzipan to shape tiny hats and scarves, pressing them into the fondant icing to secure. Shape and secure pointed noses in orange marzipan. Pipe eyes, mouths and buttons using the black icing.

Chocolate mint cake pops

Makes: 26–28
Prep: 1 hour, plus setting
Cook: 5 minutes

- 300 g/10½ oz plain chocolate, roughly chopped
- 25 g/1 oz unsalted butter, softened
- 50 g/1¾ oz hard-boiled mint sweets
- 450 g/1 lb milk chocolate
- 50 g/1¾ oz mini marshmallows, roughly chopped
- 26–28 lolly sticks
- chocolate sprinkles, to decorate

This is a cake pop version of 'rocky road', and is about as easy to make as it gets! The milk chocolate coating has family appeal, but you can use plain chocolate instead for a more adult flavour.

1. Line a baking tray with baking paper. Put the plain chocolate in a heatproof bowl, set the bowl over a saucepan of gently simmering water and heat until melted. Stir in the butter. Leave until the mixture is cool but not beginning to set.

2. Put the mint sweets in a polythene bag and tap firmly with a rolling pin until they are broken into tiny pieces. Finely chop 150 g/5½ oz of the milk chocolate, then stir it into the melted plain chocolate with the mints and marshmallows until thoroughly mixed.

3. As soon as the mixture is firm enough to hold its shape, roll 20 g/¾ oz of it into a ball. Shape the remaining cake pops in the same way. Place them on the baking tray and chill for 30–60 minutes, until firm but not brittle. Push a lolly stick into each cake pop, then chill for 10 minutes.

4. Roughly chop the remaining milk chocolate and melt as above, then remove from the heat. Dip a cake pop into the chocolate, turning it until coated. Lift it from the bowl, letting the excess drip back into the bowl, and place it in a cup or tumbler. Sprinkle with chocolate sprinkles. Repeat with the remaining cake pops. Chill or leave in a cool place until the chocolate has set.

2

3

4

Chocolate 'ice-cream' cones

Makes: 16

Prep: 40 minutes, plus setting

These mini chocolate cones are filled with a delicious chocolate mousse and topped with swirls of whipped cream. Unlike regular ice-creams, they won't melt if left out of the freezer!

125 g/4½ oz milk chocolate, roughly chopped

200 ml/7 fl oz double cream

2 tbsp vanilla sugar

chocolate and rainbow sugar sprinkles, to decorate

MOUSSE

200 g/7 oz plain chocolate, roughly chopped

4 tbsp water

2 egg whites

25 g/1 oz caster sugar

1. Line a baking tray with baking paper. To shape the cones, cut 8 circles of baking paper using a 17-cm/7-inch plate or cake tin as a guide. Fold the circles in half and then cut them in half just to one side of the fold. Shape each semi-circle into a cone so the straight edges meet to create a cone of double thickness paper, securing it in place with sticky tape.

2. Put the milk chocolate in a heatproof bowl, set the bowl over a pan of gently simmering water and heat until melted. Place a teaspoon of melted chocolate into a cone so that it's about a third full and spread the chocolate up the sides using a pastry brush. Invert it onto the baking tray and chill for at least 30 minutes, until set.

3. To make the mousse, put the plain chocolate and water in a heatproof bowl, set the bowl over a pan of gently simmering water and heat until melted. Whisk the egg whites in a clean mixing bowl until peaking. Whisk in the caster sugar, a little at a time. Tip the melted chocolate onto the whites and fold together with a spatula. Spoon the mousse into the cones and chill for 1 hour.

4. Whip the cream with the vanilla sugar until only just peaking. Put it into a small piping bag fitted with a 1-cm/½-inch star nozzle. Peel the paper from the cones and pipe swirls of cream on top. Scatter with sprinkles.

1

2

3

Double chocolate whoopie pies

Makes: 12–14
Prep: 25 minutes, plus cooling
Cook: 10 minutes

70 g/2½ oz lightly salted butter, softened

125 g/4½ oz light muscovado sugar

1 egg

1 tsp vanilla extract

125 g/4½ oz plain flour

½ tsp bicarbonate of soda

40 g/1½ oz cocoa powder

150 ml/5 fl oz buttermilk

FILLING

200 g/7 oz milk chocolate, roughly chopped

140 g/5 oz unsalted butter, softened

85 g/3 oz icing sugar

70 g/2½ oz plain chocolate, roughly chopped

chocolate sprinkles, optional

Quench your chocolate craving with these moist and morish homemade whoopies; they're so good they'll be gone before you know it!

1. Preheat the oven to 200°C/400°F/Gas Mark 6. Line 2 baking trays with baking paper. Put the lightly salted butter, light muscovado sugar, egg and vanilla in a mixing bowl and beat together with an electric handheld whisk until the mixture is thickened and pale.

2. Sift the flour, bicarbonate of soda and cocoa into a separate mixing bowl. Add half of this mixture and half the buttermilk to the butter mixture. Stir with a spatula or large metal spoon. Once combined, add the remaining flour mixture and buttermilk and carefully stir again.

3. Put the mixture into a large piping bag fitted with a 1-cm/½-inch plain nozzle (see page 8). Pipe small blobs onto the baking trays, slicing off the peaks with a small knife and spacing the blobs about 5 cm/2 inches apart to allow for expansion.

4. Bake in the preheated oven for 10 minutes, or until risen and just firm to the touch, switching over the baking trays halfway through cooking. Leave on the trays for 5 minutes, then transfer to a wire rack to cool.

5. For the filling, put the milk chocolate in a heatproof bowl, set the bowl over a saucepan of gently simmering water and heat until melted. Leave to cool slightly. Put the unsalted butter and icing sugar in a mixing bowl and beat with an electric handheld whisk until light and fluffy. Stir the melted chocolate into the butter mixture until evenly combined.

6. Sandwich the whoopie pies together in pairs with the filling. Melt the plain chocolate as above, then drizzle a little of it over each whoopie pie. Scatter with the sprinkles, if using. Leave in a cool place to firm up for a couple of hours.

Gingerbread and vanilla whoopie pies

Makes: 14
Prep: 25 minutes, plus cooling
Cook: 10 minutes

- 1 egg
- 70 g/2½ oz light muscovado sugar
- 1 tbsp black treacle
- 40 g/1½ oz lightly salted butter, melted
- 5 tbsp milk
- 150 g/5 oz plain flour
- ½ tsp bicarbonate of soda
- 1½ tsp ground ginger
- ½ tsp ground mixed spice

FILLING

- 100 g/3½ oz cream cheese
- 15 g/½ oz unsalted butter, softened
- 1 tsp vanilla extract
- 55 g/2 oz icing sugar, plus extra for dusting
- 1 tsp boiling water

These whoopies have a distinctive gingerbread flavour, perfect for autumnal comfort eating!

1. Preheat the oven to 180°C/350°F/Gas Mark 4. Line 2 baking trays with baking paper. Put the egg, light muscovado sugar and treacle in a mixing bowl and beat together with an electric handheld whisk until thickened and foamy. Beat in the lightly salted butter and milk.

2. Sift the flour, bicarbonate of soda, ginger and mixed spice into the bowl and stir with a wooden spoon to make a soft paste.

3. Spoon teaspoons of the mixture onto the baking trays, flattening them slightly so each spoonful is about 3 cm/1¼ inches in diameter. Space the spoonfuls about 5 cm/2 inches apart to allow for expansion.

4. Bake in the preheated oven for 10 minutes, or until risen and firm to the touch, switching over the baking trays halfway through cooking. Leave on the trays for 5 minutes, then transfer to a wire rack to cool.

5. For the filling, put the cream cheese, unsalted butter, vanilla and icing sugar in a mixing bowl and beat together with an electric handheld whisk until smooth and creamy. Beat in the boiling water to soften. Sandwich the whoopie pies together in pairs with the filling. Leave in a cool place to firm up for a couple of hours, then dust with icing sugar.

3

5

Index